## Back Shelf Beauties

*Bary,*
*I hope you enjoy the book and the movies!*
*Millie Waffle*

Mary,
Hope you are
enjoying the books.
The movies will be
[illegible]

# Back Shelf Beauties

♦

## Movies You Should Rent When The New Stuff Is Gone

*By Willie Waffle of*
*WaffleMovies.com*

Writer's Showcase
New York  Lincoln  Shanghai

# Back Shelf Beauties
## Movies You Should Rent When The New Stuff Is Gone

All Rights Reserved © 2002 by Willie Waffle

No part of this book may be reproduced or transmitted in any form or by any means, graphic, electronic, or mechanical, including photocopying, recording, taping, or by any information storage retrieval system, without the written permission of the publisher.

Writer's Showcase
an imprint of iUniverse, Inc.

For information address:
iUniverse, Inc.
2021 Pine Lake Road, Suite 100
Lincoln, NE 68512
www.iuniverse.com

ISBN: 0-595-25744-5 (pbk)
ISBN: 0-595-65302-2 (cloth)

Printed in the United States of America

# Contents

Preface ............................................................. xi

## Before They Were Stars

The Conversation .................................................. 3
Starring Gene Hackman and Harrison Ford

Heavy ................................................................ 5
Starring Liv Tyler, Shelley Winters, Deborah Harry and Pruitt Taylor Vince

The Man in the Moon ............................................ 8
Starring Reese Witherspoon, Jason London and Sam Waterston

Six Degrees of Separation ....................................... 10
Starring Will Smith, Stockard Channing, Donald Sutherland and Heather Graham

American Flyers .................................................... 13
Starring Kevin Costner, David Grant, Rae Dawn Chong, Alexandra Paul and John Amos

Mississippi Masala ................................................. 16
Starring Denzel Washington

Gallipoli .............................................................. 18
Starring Mel Gibson

Marvin's Room ..................................................... 20
Starring Meryl Streep, Diane Keaton, Leonardo DiCaprio and Robert De Niro

Mystic Pizza . . . . . . . . . . . . . . . . . . . . . . . . . . . . . . . . . . . . . . . . . . 22
Starring Julia Roberts

## The Forgotten Films

Looking for Richard . . . . . . . . . . . . . . . . . . . . . . . . . . . . . . . . . . . 27
Starring Al Pacino, Kevin Spacey, Winona Ryder and Alec Baldwin

The Spanish Prisoner . . . . . . . . . . . . . . . . . . . . . . . . . . . . . . . . . 29
Starring Campbell Scott and Steve Martin

In Country . . . . . . . . . . . . . . . . . . . . . . . . . . . . . . . . . . . . . . . . . . 31
Starring Bruce Willis, Emily Lloyd and Joan Allen

Shout . . . . . . . . . . . . . . . . . . . . . . . . . . . . . . . . . . . . . . . . . . . . . . . 34
Starring John Travolta, James Walters, Heather Graham and Gwyneth Paltrow

Welcome to Sarajevo . . . . . . . . . . . . . . . . . . . . . . . . . . . . . . . . . 37
Starring Woody Harrelson, Stephen Dillane and Marisa Tomei

Finding Graceland . . . . . . . . . . . . . . . . . . . . . . . . . . . . . . . . . . . 40
Starring Harvey Keitel, Jonathan Schaech and Bridget Fonda

Election . . . . . . . . . . . . . . . . . . . . . . . . . . . . . . . . . . . . . . . . . . . . 43
Starring Reese Witherspoon and Matthew Broderick

American Buffalo . . . . . . . . . . . . . . . . . . . . . . . . . . . . . . . . . . . 46
Starring Dennis Franz and Dustin Hoffman

Two Bits . . . . . . . . . . . . . . . . . . . . . . . . . . . . . . . . . . . . . . . . . . . . 49
Starring Al Pacino, Jerry Barone and Mary Elizabeth Mastrantonio

Mad City . . . . . . . . . . . . . . . . . . . . . . . . . . . . . . . . . . . . . . . . . . . 52
Starring John Travolta and Dustin Hoffman

The Hudsucker Proxy . . . . . . . . . . . . . . . . . . . . . . . . . . . . . . . . 55
Starring Tim Robbins, Paul Newman and Jennifer Jason Leigh

## The Classics

The Desperate Hours . . . . . . . . . . . . . . . . . . . . . . . . . . . . . 61
Starring Humphrey Bogart and Frederic March

It Happened One Night . . . . . . . . . . . . . . . . . . . . . . . . . . . 64
Starring Clark Gable and Claudette Colbert

A Patch of Blue. . . . . . . . . . . . . . . . . . . . . . . . . . . . . . . . . . 67
Starring Sydney Poitier, Shelley Winters and Elizabeth Hartman

Marty . . . . . . . . . . . . . . . . . . . . . . . . . . . . . . . . . . . . . . . . . 70
Starring Earnest Borgnine

A Guy Named Joe. . . . . . . . . . . . . . . . . . . . . . . . . . . . . . . . 73
Starring Spencer Tracy, Irene Dunn and Van Johnson

Angels in the Outfield. . . . . . . . . . . . . . . . . . . . . . . . . . . . 75
Starring Paul Douglas and Janet Leigh

Broadcast News. . . . . . . . . . . . . . . . . . . . . . . . . . . . . . . . . 78
Starring Holly Hunter, William Hurt, Albert Brooks and Jack Nicholson

Horse Feathers . . . . . . . . . . . . . . . . . . . . . . . . . . . . . . . . . 81
Starring The Marx Brothers

The Mouse That Roared. . . . . . . . . . . . . . . . . . . . . . . . . 83
Starring Peter Sellers

Dr. Jeckyll and Mr. Hyde . . . . . . . . . . . . . . . . . . . . . . . . 86
Starring Spencer Tracy, Ingrid Bergman and Lana Turner

The Hand. . . . . . . . . . . . . . . . . . . . . . . . . . . . . . . . . . . . . 89
Starring Michael Caine

Never Cry Wolf . . . . . . . . . . . . . . . . . . . . . . . . . . . . . . . . 91
Starring Charles Martin Smith

The Great Santini . . . . . . . . . . . . . . . . . . . . . . . . . . . . . . 93
Starring Robert Duvall, Blythe Danner and Michael O'Keefe

Christmas Eve . . . . . . . . . . . . . . . . . . . . . . . . . . . . . . . . . . . . . . . . . . . . . 96
Starring Loretta Young

Holiday Affair . . . . . . . . . . . . . . . . . . . . . . . . . . . . . . . . . . . . . . . . . . . . 99
Starring Robert Mitchum and Janet Leigh

# The Independents

Just Write . . . . . . . . . . . . . . . . . . . . . . . . . . . . . . . . . . . . . . . . . . . . . . 103
Starring Jeremy Piven and Sherilyn Fenn

Rosewood . . . . . . . . . . . . . . . . . . . . . . . . . . . . . . . . . . . . . . . . . . . . . 106
Starring Ving Rhames, Don Cheadle, Esther Rolle and Jon Voight

The Gun in Betty Lou's Handbag . . . . . . . . . . . . . . . . . . . . . . . 109
Starring Penelope Ann Miller and Alfre Woodard

Grace of My Heart . . . . . . . . . . . . . . . . . . . . . . . . . . . . . . . . . . . . . 112
Starring Illeana Douglas, Matt Dillon, John Turturro and Patsy Kensit

This is My Father . . . . . . . . . . . . . . . . . . . . . . . . . . . . . . . . . . . . . 115
Starring James Caan, Aidan Quinn, Moya Farrelly and Colm Meaney

The Imposters . . . . . . . . . . . . . . . . . . . . . . . . . . . . . . . . . . . . . . . . 117
Starring Stanley Tucci, Oliver Platt, Hope Davis, Steve Buscemi and Tony Shalhoub

Waiting for Guffman . . . . . . . . . . . . . . . . . . . . . . . . . . . . . . . . . . 119
Starring Christopher Guest, Eugene Levy, Parker Posey and Catherine O'Hara

Swingers . . . . . . . . . . . . . . . . . . . . . . . . . . . . . . . . . . . . . . . . . . . . . 121
Starring Jon Favreau, Vince Vaughn and Heather Graham

A Walk on the Moon . . . . . . . . . . . . . . . . . . . . . . . . . . . . . . . . . . 124
Starring Diane Lane, Liev Schreiber and Viggo Mortenson

Big Night . . . . . . . . . . . . . . . . . . . . . . . . . . . . . . . . . . . . . . . . . . . . 126
Starring Stanley Tucci, Tony Shalhoub, Minnie Driver and Allison Janney

Ulee's Gold ............................................. 129
Starring Peter Fonda, Patricia Richardson and Jessica Biel

Brassed Off ............................................. 132
Starring Pete Postlethwaite, Ewan McGregor and Tara Fitzgerald

Jawbreaker ............................................. 135
Starring Rose McGowan and Rebecca Gayheart

The Apostle ............................................. 137
Starring Robert Duvall and Farrah Fawcett

The DayTrippers ......................................... 139
Starring Hope Davis, Stanley Tucci, Anne Meara, Liev Shreiber and Parker Posey

Shall We Dance? ......................................... 142
Hideko Kara and Yo Tokui

Matewan ............................................... 144
Starring Chris Cooper, Kevin Tighe, and Gordon Clapp

The Woman In Black ..................................... 147
Starring Adrian Rawlins and Pauline Moran

# *Preface*

A few years ago, I was a public relations consultant and knew I wanted to do something else. This feeling grew over the course of several months, until the night I came to a decision. Why spend my life doing something that only made other people rich. I loved movies and my friends were always asking me what I thought about this film or that film. Even my roommate, Brian, suggested that I start reviewing films. So I did.

I decided to start a web site, ***www.wafflemovies.com***, where movie lovers could go to find out about movies that they never heard of, didn't know much about, or didn't know were available on video and DVD. These Back Shelf Beauties were collecting dust instead of entertaining people. While I have never made a lot of money doing it, this has been my most rewarding work. The site evolved over the years and I started reviewing new releases for WMAL radio and FOX 5 TV here in DC, but I think I will come back to the old, forgotten movies again someday.

I don't have a film school background. I don't even live in Hollywood. But I love the magic, wonder and inspiration of movies. That's what this book is all about.

Thanks for buying my book. I hope you will enjoy the selections.

# Acknowledgements

I have been very lucky throughout my life to have family and friends who support my crazy ideas and dreams. This section is the hardest to write because I don't want to leave anyone out.

Thank you to everyone who ever suggested a movie to me. This includes folks like Kristina Blankenship, Victoria Jones, Michele Novy, Joy Nagel, Mary Hewitt, Paul Cummins, Bob McCarson, Dan Leonard, Bianca Zinzi, Rob and Carolyn Durell, Susan Monday, Mike Cremedas, Scott Wykoff, Brian Bernhardt, Mark Carr, James Lanyon and many others. In a way, they are the unofficial advisory committee to WaffleMovies.com. Many of the movies appear in this book, so they should buy a copy!

Thank you to my family, especially my father Bill, my mother Darlene and sister Tina. I never told them that I started my web site until I had the radio gig. Somehow I didn't think they would believe it until I had some proof that someone wanted to hear what I had to say about movies.

Thank you to my friend Brian Fauls. He has suggested movies, listened to my rants about what is wrong with the world and Hollywood, spread the word about the site, and put up with my sloppiness when we shared an apartment. I can't say enough about what a great guy he is. Plus, if any of the women reading this book are looking for a good man, he's single and looking.

Thank you to Bob Moppert, who gave me a job that started my move to Washington, DC as well as some of the best advice about life that I have ever gotten. Thank you to Jerry Klein, who doesn't realize that he motivated me to finish this book.

Thank you to Andrea Perry and Chris Core at WMAL-AM 630 in Washington, DC for taking a chance on me. They gave me my first radio interview and thought I was good enough to bring back every week to review what is new in the video stores. I did that for over 2 years, and honed the skills (or lack of skills) that I have now. Without them, I never would be at this point in my careeer.

Thank you to Tim Brant, Andy Parks, John Butler and Dan Loukota who liked me enough on The Chris Core Show to have me join WMAL-AM 630's morning show to review what's new at the cineplex. I wish it could have continued forever.

Thank you to the Saturday Morning posse on WMAL—David Burd, Mike "Satan" Cremedas and Andrew O'Day. When the station changed and I didn't "fit" with the other shows anymore, David brought me over to his Saturday morning program, and gave me new life. David, Mike and Andrew have been my friends, my confidantes and my supporters. Some of my best and happiest moments are Saturday mornings.

Thank you to all the producers and hosts who have interviewed me including Victoria Jones, Tina Chapa, Kristin Nash, Charlie Warren, Debbie Rochon, Tim Reid, and Brooke Stevens. I'll be calling you to help promote the book.

When I started writing this dedication, I thought I could keep it to one page, but something magical happened. FOX 5 in Washington, DC called me to appear on their FOX 5 Morning News to review the newest movies at the cineplex. So thank you to Patricia Corchoran, Mike Garguilo, Lark McCarthy, Sean Yancey, Allison Seymour, Holly Morris, Tom Sater (the guy who gets my jokes) and the entire staff at WTTG-TV.

Most of all, thank you to everyone who reads WaffleMovies.com, gets my weekly newsletter, watched me on TV or listens to me on the radio. Without you, I would be nowhere

*Before They Were Stars*

# *The Conversation*

◆

## *Starring Gene Hackman and Harrison Ford*

Simply put, this is one of the best movies of the seventies. Gene Hackman stars as Harry Caul, a legendary surveillance expert. He has been hired to follow a young couple and record their conversation in the park for a powerful and dangerous man, but Caul isn't quite sure why he has been hired or what he is after, so he struggles to make sense of the conversation. Soon, he discovers that the young couple is in danger.

For Caul, this seems to be déjà vu all over again. He is legendary for work he performed in New York, but feels guilty because the case led to the murder of three people. It still haunts him, and Caul fears the same thing will happen in this case. An intensely private man, he soon finds the tables have been turned, and he is the target of surveillance.

***Will he be able to protect the young couple and himself from this mysterious and dangerous client?***

Some of the greatest talent in film came together for this prolific movie. Written and directed by Francis Ford Coppola, the film is full of suspense and plot twists that will keep you guessing. Coppola provides a script that challenges the audience to follow along and play detective. Modern audiences are used to a faster moving and more predictable film, but if you exercise some patience and follow closely, the surprise ending makes this an enjoyable movie.

A great script can't survive without great acting, so Coppola assembled a fantastic cast of veterans and up-and-coming stars. Hackman is fabulous as the paranoid, brilliant and suspicious Harry Caul. He gives the character depth by portraying his guilt in a tender, vulnerable way while also showing how good he is at the job.

In one of his earliest roles, Harrison Ford plays Martin Stett, the client's menacing assistant who tries to keep Caul away from the boss. Ford does a great job of being quietly intimidating. He plays the character with a self-assurance that intimidates Caul without over-doing it. Instead of yelling and flexing his muscle, Stett controls Caul with a cold stare and strange charisma. Maybe Harrison used this power to woo the young Calista Flockhart as well? And if he did, could he teach the power to me? I am not above dating young, beautiful women.

You'll also recognize several other prominent actors. John Cazale, best known as Fredo in *The Godfather*, plays Caul's assistant who resents Harry's protectiveness of his privacy and trade secrets. Teri Garr plays Caul's girlfriend, and Cindy Williams of *Laverne and Shirley* fame plays the young lady in danger. Also, watch for a surprise appearance by a famous actor in the role of Caul's powerful client.

With so much worry about personal privacy in the computer age, Coppola is a visionary by investigating the themes of privacy and the ways our most personal conversations and behaviors can be monitored. Imagine what he could do if he updated the movie to include computer hackers, which didn't exist when it first came out.

If you're in the mood for a good suspenseful movie, rent *The Conversation*.

# *Heavy*

### *Starring Liv Tyler, Shelley Winters, Deborah Harry and Pruitt Taylor Vince*

I tend to like movies that don't jump out at you. It's fun to see a big, loud special effects-laden blockbuster, but sometimes you need a subtle, quiet movie that makes you think. *Heavy* is just that sort of thinking person's movie.

Pruitt Taylor Vince stars as Victor, the overweight, shy and caring cook at his mother's (Shelley Winters) diner. The diner is a place where nothing changes. It is filled with people who feel life has beaten them and taken away their hopes and dreams. They quietly live out their bleak existence while sipping coffee or downing too much alcohol. Victor is an example of how little these people expect out of life.

Although he is an adult, he has never grown up. He lives a sheltered life taking care of his mother and the diner. He is an unassuming man who keeps to himself and never expresses the deep sadness that lies behind those expressive eyes. As one of the characters points out, he is as, "big as an ox but no one sees [him]." Victor never dreams about having much more out of life, until Callie (Liv Tyler) enters it.

Callie is a young woman who doesn't know where she is going in life. She drops out of college and lives with her wannabe-rock star boyfriend (Evan Dando). She decides to take a job at the diner and quickly warms to Victor because she sees a potential in Victor that no one else has ever sought out. She recognizes his love for cooking and tries to get him to go to the local culinary school to pursue a career as a chef, but his mother mocks the idea wondering why she should pay for him to learn what he already knows. His mother doesn't understand that there is an entire world outside of the diner, but Callie has shown Victor that he can have more.

Victor falls in love with Callie and decides to shape up in an attempt to become more attractive. He starts to exercise and eat less, but he is soon forced to face adulthood and his future for the first time.

***Will he be able to keep the diner running, maintain his new lifestyle and learn to live on his own?***

***Can he express his true love to Callie or is he too afraid of change?***

Pruitt Taylor Vince will amaze you with his subtle, but powerful portrayal of the lovable Victor. Vince has very few lines, which shows how shy his character is, but expresses the character's feelings with his eyes, facial expressions and physical mannerisms. He captivates you without saying a word and draws you into his world. I have seen Vince in other roles, and this is his best. He is a talented actor who would be a household name and perennial Oscar nominee if he had the looks of Tom Cruise or Paul Newman. On the other hand, we have the beautiful actress destined for stardom due to her looks.

Liv Tyler shines in this movie, made just before she became the big star of *Stealing Beauty, Armageddon* and *That Thing You Do*. She is wonderful as the caring, but confused young lady. Victor is drawn to Callie for more than just her pouty good looks (although the pouty lips don't hurt). Tyler portrays her tenderness and caring for Victor, as well as the frustration Callie feels about her own life. She witnesses the despair around her and wonders if she too is destined to live a painful, uneventful life. It would have been easy for the character to become very whiny, but Tyler fleshes out the character to make her likable and strong.

The two leads are supported by great performances from Shelley Winters as Dolly, the mother who loves and shelters Victor too much, and Deborah "Blondie" Harry as Delores, the life long waitress with no future. The knock against Winters has always been her nature to play characters very loudly and over the top. However, her performance in this movie is a nice change of pace. She brings emotional depth to the character instead of playing the stereotypical overbearing mother.

I don't know how Writer/Director James Mangold convinced Deborah Harry to take this part, but I am glad he did. The punk/new wave superstar is wonderful as the frustrated and angry Delores. She feuds with Dolly and resents the presence of the younger and more beautiful Callie. In many ways, you feel Delores was just like Callie years ago. Callie also senses this and hopes never to end up like Delores.

Get some ice cream and enjoy Heavy this weekend.

# The Man in the Moon

✦

## *Starring Reese Witherspoon, Jason London and Sam Waterston*

Summer lovin', had me a blast.

Summer lovin' happened so fast.

Yes, summer is the time for young love. Everyone remembers his or her first love. It's a time of innocence and wonder as you explore new emotions and mature into adulthood. *The Man in the Moon* is a touching tearjerker that documents one young lady's coming of age and her first experience with this powerful emotion.

Young Danni (Reese Witherspoon) is a typical 14-year old young lady in the late 1950's. She's a tomboy, dreams of Elvis, is starting to wonder about love, and is slowly maturing into a woman. Danni has a special relationship with her older sister, 17-year old Maureen (Emily Warfield). The prettiest and smartest girl in school, Maureen has the world at her doorstep. Every boy wants to date her, and she has earned a scholarship to Duke University (without the ability to hit a 3-pointer or crossover dribble, so she must be smart). However, Maureen yearns for true love that, "sweeps you away." Don't we all.

One day, Danni goes swimming in a pond close to her home. While frolicking in the water, a new 17-year old stranger joins her. It is pure hate at first sight as Court (Jason London) accuses Danni of trespassing on his land. Embarrassed and angry, Danni retreats to her family home, but you know how hate and loathing in the films leads to something else.

### *Will Danni be able to win Court's heart?*

Most movies today that star young people tend to lack the kind of charm and innocence that makes this movie such a wonderful find. Today's teen movies are filled with smart aleck, know-it-all pubescents with no heart and soul. Made in 1990, *The Man in the Moon* was produced before this current crop of heartless movies came into fashion.

Another refreshing aspect of the movie is its portrayal of adults. Today, movies geared to and starring teens tend to reduce adults to unflattering stereotypical shrews and dunces. However, the adults in this film are loving, respectable, protective and wise. Sam Waterston is fantastic as the strong father trying to protect his daughters, while also allowing them to grow. Tess Harper also deserves kudos as the pregnant mother of three helping her daughters face a changing world, while struggling with her own problems.

I warn everyone that you should buy a box of tissues on your way home from the video store, maybe two boxes if you are the emotional type. The movie marks the premiere of Reese Witherspoon and shows what great talent she has. It is a role with great depth, spanning jealously to wonder to confusion. While putting in a tremendous overall performance, especially for such a young kid, Witherspoon is particularly captivating late in the movie as she fights for a love she knows she can't win. It is painful to watch her fight for Court even though she thinks he is lost. The fact that we have all been there makes it even more poignant as we recognize her anguish.

This was the last film from famed director Robert Mulligan. Even though he was born in the Bronx, Mulligan had a great ability to translate southern-style storytelling to the screen. He achieved great fame and praise with 1962's masterpiece, *To Kill a Mockingbird*. You'll see many of the same elements of southern literature in *The Man in The Moon*.

I hope you will enjoy this film as much as I do. Be warned, it is a tearjerker.

# Six Degrees of Separation

◆

## Starring Will Smith, Stockard Channing, Donald Sutherland and Heather Graham

Before he saved the world from aliens in *Men in Black* and *Independence Day* and she became the world's most shagadelic superspy *in Austin Powers II: The Spy Who Shagged Me*, Will Smith and Heather Graham starred in this true story of a young man living on the hospitality of rich New Yorkers while claiming to be the son of Sydney Poitier. This tale of vanity and the phoniness of the upper crust of society is a wonderful rental for those who want to see a movie from the king of the July 4th weekend, Will Smith.

The movie opens with a business dinner between Geoffrey (Ian McKellen), Flanders (Donald Sutherland) and Ouisa (Stockard Channing). Flanders is an ethically challenged art dealer who desperately needs to complete a deal, and must have a $2 million investment from Geoffrey to succeed. The evening takes an unexpected turn when young Paul (Smith) shows up at the door claiming to be a friend of his children and suffering a knife wound from a mugging. Paul claims he is the son of famous actor Sydney Poitier and needs a place to stay until he meets his father the next morning. Paul charms the group with his intelligent conversation, masterful cooking and stories of his father. The evening is perfect, until Ouisa catches Paul in a compromising situation in their apartment and chases him away.

The next day, Flanders and Ouisa must hurry to a wedding and are excited about the chance to tell the magnificent story to their snooty friends. However, Ouisa and Flanders soon run into Larkin (Bruce

Davison) and Kitty (Mary Beth Hurt) who tell the same remarkable story. The group goes on a mission to find out if this mysterious stranger really is the son of Sydney Poitier. Along the way, they must confront their own strained familial relations and the emptiness of their own lives.

### What is the truth?

This is a true story that occurred on New York's East Side in the eighties, and it was soon turned into a play starring Stockard Channing, who justifiably had the opportunity to star in the movie version. Luckily, she is joined by a stellar ensemble.

Before he stunned the world with his portrayal of Muhammed Ali, this movie was the Will Smith movie to show that he is a wonderful actor. While his most famous parts are in action/adventure movies, he has great range, which is on display in this movie. Smith is able to glide gracefully between scenes where is character is charming and amiable to other scenes where he shows his steely dark side. As Smith grows older, I think you will see him take more of these challenging films and will, someday, win an Oscar.

Another actor who surprises is eighties teen movie idol Anthony Michael Hall. Hall plays a role crucial to the plot, so I won't give too much away. However, I will tell you that you won't recognize the same Hall you are accustomed to in movies like *The Breakfast Club*. He transforms himself into this darker role. Along with his recent performance in TNT's *Pirates of Silicon Valley*, Hall has a strong resume to shop around Hollywood as he looks to revive his career.

Of course, I must mention Heather Graham, who you might not even recognize as young, midwesterner Elizabeth. She puts in a great performance as the naïve, but quickly maturing victim of a scam. Along with her performance as Roller Girl in *Boogie Nights*, she also shows an acting ability that should be nurtured even as she tries to recover from becoming the latest "it" girl to make bad choices in follow up movies.

Like the famous Kevin Bacon game (where I am 3, count 'em, 3 degrees from Kevin Bacon. One degree if you count the time we met in a hallway), the movie tries to make the point that we are all just six degrees of separation from anyone else, so we should try to treat each other in a more civil and caring way. While the overall theme is lost in the movie, it is a great evening of entertainment and a chance to see some of the greatest actors in Hollywood.

# *American Flyers*

*Starring Kevin Costner, David Grant, Rae Dawn Chong, Alexandra Paul and John Amos*

Sometimes, we all need a little sinful indulgence. Ben and Jerry have made millions off this need, so has Mrs. Fields (and both should thank me for my SIGNIFICANT contributions to their fortunes). View the movie *American Flyers* as your sinful indulgence. It isn't going to change the world and doesn't make any great social commentary. It is just a pure 80's cliché. It includes a dysfunctional family, youthful rebellion, a synthesizer driven rock and roll soundtrack full of inspirational tunes, even a subplot involving the U.S. boycott of the 1980 Olympics and one athlete's bitterness over not getting his chance at Olympic glory. It even has Kevin Costner with a cheesy 80's mustache! It is an enjoyable movie that doesn't take itself too seriously, so you shouldn't either.

The movie stars David Grant as bicyclist David Sommers. After the tragic death of his father, David has lost focus, done poorly in school and watched his family disintegrate. His own mortality looms largely in his thoughts because his father died from a cerebral aneurysm, a weak blood vessel in the brain that can't be fixed and is hereditary.

His father's death also strained the relationship between his mother (Janice Rule) and brother, Marcus (Kevin Costner). Marcus is a doctor who resents his mother's inability to face reality and comfort his father during the final days. Marcus also wants his brother to join him in

Madison to get an education, get away from his mother and pursue his athletic ability. He secretly worries that his brother may develop a similar cerebral aneurysm, and wants to examine him with the school's cutting edge equipment before it is too late.

We soon learn that Marcus also has a past. He was a champion bicyclist, serving as an alternate for the 1980 Olympic team. However, he is disappointed with his performance. Marcus feels he always gave up and wasn't driven enough. He regrets what could have been a fantastic career. To make up for it, he is traveling to Colorado for a prestigious bike race. After the race, Marcus plans on retiring from competition.

### *Who will win the big race?*

I have always been a big fan of Kevin Costner. In most roles (not *Waterworld* or *The Postman*), he is a natural, almost effortless actor, much like Spencer Tracy. He always comes across as a regular guy trying to do what's right for himself, his family or his friends. This has helped Costner survive suicidal career choices and star in some of the best movies of the last twenty years. His career always seems to be feast (*Bull Durham, Dances With Wolves*) or famine (*Dragonfly*).

In *American Flyers*, Costner's character is trying to instill pride in his brother and push him to succeed. It's not an overbearing nagging, but a loving push to be all you can be. Costner portrays a tough, but lovable older brother. It's a hard balancing act, but he is very good at it.

Most of the other performances are very stereotyped. However, two other actors stand out, Rae Dawn Chong as Marcus' girlfriend and John Amos as Dennis. Chong portrays a tough as nails, loving girlfriend who defends her man and pushes him when he is wrong. Amos is fantastic as the older best friend trying to give good advice to a headstrong young man. I have always liked Amos since he was on television's *Good Times*, and wish he would get more work. Maybe Aaron Sorkin can include him in more episodes of *The West Wing*! Watch for three actors who are well known now, but were just getting started then; Jennifer Grey of *Dirty Dancing*, comedian Robert Townsend and Alexandra Paul of *Baywatch*.

As I mentioned, the movie is unabashedly cliché, right up to the dramatic big race, but that's OK. As a child of the eighties, I enjoyed the trip down memory lane.

# *Mississippi Masala*

✦

## *Starring Denzel Washington*

I originally reviewed this film for Valentine's Day. While I vehemently oppose this evil attempt by multi-national corporations to make billions of dollars off the common man by filling his wife's or girlfriend's head with the silly idea that love must be expressed on one specific, make-or-break, show-me-you love-me-or-else day of the year (yeah, I don't have a girlfriend and I'm bitter), I do like a good romance from time to time. Mississippi Masala, starring Denzel Washington, is one that I enjoy.

Denzel stars as Dimitrius, a hard working carpet cleaning business owner in Greenwood, Mississippi. He has had difficulty getting his business up and running, and he must take care of his out of work brother and elderly father, so money is tight. On top of all that, Dimitrius has been nursing a broken heart since his girlfriend left town.

One fateful day, Dimitrius' truck is hit from behind by Meena (Sarita Choudhury), a beautiful, 24 year old, Indian (that's a gal from India) lady. She feels very sorry, but, thank the stars above for small favors, he gets her phone number. Soon, they are dating, having a good time and falling in love.

***Will their love survive when Meena's family objects to her interracial dating?***

Unfortunately, I disagree with the film's structure. If I could re-edit the movie, I would make a few changes. We learn at the beginning of the film that Meena's family was expelled from Uganda in 1972, when dictator Idi Amin forcibly removed all non-Africans from the country and took their land. It's a heart-breaking tale, and central to our understanding of her father's, Jay (Roshan Seth), resistance to Dimitrius. However, I think director Mira Nair should have saved this information for later to heighten it's dramatic effect.

However, the film is full of good acting performances. Of course, Denzel is awesome. You expected different? He brings fire and passion to the character, while also showing us a vulnerable and loving side. His struggles endear him to the audience as he is able to play on our emotions. You want to root for this underdog.

Choudhury tends to overact in some key moments due to a limited range, but Roshan Seth shines as her father, Jay. We learn that Jay lost almost everything he ever loved. Although he is of Indian descent, he was born and raised in Uganda. His family, friends and life were taken away from him in 1972. This helps us understand why he doesn't like Dimitrius, but writer Sooni Taraporevala should have developed more tension between Dimitrius, Jay and other characters to make the audience believe that they wouldn't get along.

Overall, rent the movie for the Romeo and Juliet tale and Denzel's usual fantastic performance.

# *Gallipoli*

✦

## *Starring Mel Gibson*

He is one of today's hottest hunks, but there is one Mel Gibson movie you probably missed along the way.

Back in 1981, Gibson starred as Frank, an Aussie rebel pursuing a joyful life on the homefront during World War I. Not one for sentimentality or nationalistic pride, Frank doesn't want to follow his buddies, who are itching to join the army and battle the Turks in 1915. He doesn't see the usefulness of fighting someone else's war (the Australians are dedicated to defending British interests). Along the way, he meets Archie (Mark Lee).

Archie is a runner, maybe one of the best that the country has ever seen. He trains with his uncle and strives to go to the Olympics, but the war is growing in importance. Archie feels a patriotic calling to join the army, but he is too young, and his family opposes it. Frank, moved by Archie's honest passion, decides to help him sneak into the army, and, along the way, must decide if he wants to join the fight.

*Will Frank join the army?*

*Will Archie get in?*

Gallipoli is often referred to as "The Australian Alamo" and plays a huge role in the film. Viewed by the British as a key peninsula between Asia Minor and Europe during World War I, it was Australian troops who led the bloody ground battle against the German-allied Turks, while the British attempted to attack from the sea. Unfortunately, the

British and Australians suffered from ill-fated attack plans, mistimed troop movements and serious opposition from the Turks, which led to the death of many ANZAC(Australian New Zealand Army Corps) troops.

However, the film Gallipoli is about friendship and honor. Mel Gibson, won the best actor award from the Australian Film Institute for his role, is able to embody the indecision young men face when war raises its ugly head. His character is driven by self-interest, but he feels terrible pangs of conscience when his friends join the war. He wants to defend them, and certainly doesn't want to be viewed as a coward or disloyal to his country. Eventually, it is a different loyalty that causes him to make his ultimate decision. It is a great early performance from a man who didn't get his due until 1994's *Braveheart*. He leaves the stud image at home, and becomes a complex, likable character.

Of course, *Gallipoli* is also a mature look at the decisions we make and the battles we fight. Throughout the film, we learn that the Aussies are not faring well in Gallipoli, yet, many young men choose to fight a battle that cannot be won. What drives them? The same thing that drives most us—a need to try, a need to defend something greater than ourselves, and a desire to do what's right. In the end, that's why *Gallipoli* is a winner.

# Marvin's Room

✦

## Starring Meryl Streep, Diane Keaton, Leonardo DiCaprio and Robert De Niro

You say you need your Leo fix, but your favorite neighborhood video store just ran out of copies of *The Beach*? Don't fret (actually thank your lucky stars. *The Beach* is nothing more than a bad episode of *Survivor* without the intrigue and entertainment value). Why not check out *Marvin's Room*, one of his earliest and best performances.

Diane Keaton plays Bessie, a fortyish, spinster lady who has dedicated her life to caring for her ailing father, Marvin (Hume Cronyn), and aunt. She doesn't have a husband or children of her own, so life is pretty boring. One day, she visits good old Doctor Wally (Robert DeNiro), who discovers that she has leukemia and needs a bone marrow donor to save her life. Reluctantly, she calls her estranged sister, Lee (Meryl Streep), for help.

Lee left her family behind twenty years ago for the love of her life. Unfortunately, he is no longer in the picture (can't tell you why because it is a major plot point) and she has to raise her two sons alone. Young Chuck is just fine, but Hank (Leonardo DiCaprio) has been committed to a mental institution after he burned down the family home. He doesn't get along with his Mom and desperately wants to find the father he never knew, but idolizes.

**When Bessie calls Lee, will she be able to help?**

The film could have easily become a weeper like so many movies of the week you find on NBC, CBS or Lifetime. However, writer Scott McPherson creates a touching film that also has moments of levity to keep even the most hardened guy interested. DeNiro is fabulous as the affable, quirky and bordering on incompetent doctor who tries to help Bessie through her troubles. I wish we would have had more DeNiro. Even if you hate DeNiro, check out this film to see that he can be very funny. You'll also love Dan Hedaya as Dr. Wally's even crazier brother. He's come a long way since playing Nick Tortelli on *Cheers*.

While the comedy keeps the men interested, the women are the stars of this show. Keaton is great as the woman who is losing a life that she regrets. While she loves her father and aunt, Keaton gives you the sense that Bessie wants more out of life. They have become her surrogate children since she has none of her own. She also has a wonderful chemistry with Leo.

DiCaprio does a fine job as the troubled youth who believes everyone wants something out of him and doesn't find someone to look up to until he meets Bessie. He could have gone overboard as a raging, yell-in-an-overdramatic-manner at everything, but uses more subtlety than that. Streep is just fine as the frustrated mother who finally feels life is starting to work out. Although, what the heck is that accent she is trying to use? Meryl, honey, you don't need it everytime.

# Mystic Pizza

❖

## Starring Julia Roberts

One fateful summer, writer Amy Jones was taking a summer vacation in the quiet little town of Mystic, Connecticut. As she walked down West Main Street, she came upon a local favorite, Mystic Pizza—a small, family run shop with the best pizza in the world (according to them). She was intrigued by the place, and decided to write her next film about it.

Set in this sleepy fishing town, Mystic Pizza focuses on the trials and tribulations of three (fictional) local waitresses. Daisy (Julia Roberts) is the town's foul-mouthed floozy seeking true love with a rich kid, law school student who drives around town in a Porsche. Her sister, Kat (Annabeth Gish), is the favorite child who works four jobs in an attempt to raise enough money to attend Yale. Lastly, their pal, JoJo (Lilli Taylor), is supposed to be getting married to her boyfriend, Bill (Vincent D'Onofrio), but she loves the sex more than she loves him.

*Will Daisy get her man?*

*Will JoJo marry Bill?*

*Can Kat avoid having an affair with her new boss?*

*Will the pizza place get more business so it can stay open?*

Today, a movie starring Matt Damon and Julia Roberts would be considered the next great blockbuster, but 13 years ago, they were just up-and-coming actors starring in a little, independent flick. *Mystic*

*Pizza* is a great film for the ladies, right down to the prerequisite scene of the girls celebrating sisterhood, while singing and dancing to 60's rhythm and blues tunes (Aretha, of course). Roberts is fantastic as the envious sister with nothing going for her but her good looks. Daisy is the black sheep of the family and just wants to snag a man who can get her out of town. Compared to the more cliched stories involving the other two female leads, Roberts' role and performance stand out.

Roberts shows great strength and vulnerability at appropriate times, which foreshadowed what great acting talent she has when given the chance to do some acting. When you look at Julia's filmography, for every *Erin Brockovich*, there is a *Runaway Bride*. I'd love to see her expand her repertoire, and maybe she will get the chance over the next few years.

Watch for Matt Damon in a crucial scene towards the end of the movie. If you want a good girls' night out, call up some friends, pop the popcorn and rent *Mystic Pizza*.

*The Forgotten Films*

# Looking for Richard

✦

## Starring Al Pacino, Kevin Spacey, Winona Ryder and Alec Baldwin

Al Pacino will always be remembered for his tough guy roles in *The Godfather* and *Scarface*. However, he has another side. He is a funny man with a deep passion for the classical works of William Shakespeare. In *Looking for Richard*, Pacino shares his love for the Bard while also educating us about one of his greatest plays, *Richard III*.

The movie is Pacino's effort to explain his feelings for Shakespeare and how people in the modern age can enjoy his work. As director, Pacino splices together interviews with experts, comments from people on the street, rehearsals, debates among the cast, his own practice sessions and the finished scenes to create an enjoyable and insightful investigation of the play and attitudes toward Shakespeare.

With the film, Pacino tries to dispel the myth that Shakespeare is too advanced for average people to understand. View the movie as a Cliff Notes version of the play. Shakespeare's work is often hard to understand because the writing style is much different from what we are accustomed to today. Pacino cuts through the ponderous style to explain the key scenes in layman's terms, but only early on.

As the film progresses, Pacino steps back to let the audience use the knowledge they gained early in the movie to understand and interpret the closing scenes. As they watch the movie, the audience develops this capability. I was surprised at how much more understandable the play was once I had early scenes described by Pacino and crew.

The best scenes in *Looking for Richard* show us the planning of the movie as Pacino and crew scout locations, visit key historical sites and speak with fellow actors about the play. The actors and producers analyze the meaning of the story and key scenes to enhance their own performances, while making things clearer for the audience. Also, actors explain the motivations and histories of their characters to provide the audience with the background needed to understand the story.

Another enjoyable aspect of the movie is seeing the funny, softer side of Pacino. He is one of America's greatest actors, yet, we know little about him and his personality. The audience is given a behind-the-scenes peak to see Pacino debating with the producers, mingling with friends, interacting with fans and speaking about one of his favorite writers. In many ways, the movie could also be called Looking for Al.

The audience also gets a fine performance of *Richard III*. Pacino is spell-binding in the final scenes as Richard must confront the punishment for evil actions he has committed. Winona Ryder as Anne and Alec Baldwin as Clarence also give great performances. These well known actors rarely have the opportunity to engage in widely seen theatrical work. Baldwin has participated in Broadway productions, but few had the opportunity to see them unless you were in New York.

Many of us probably remember the boring documentaries we had to watch in school, but this one is a pleasant and informative evening of entertainment led by "Professor" Pacino.

# *The Spanish Prisoner*

## *Starring Campbell Scott and Steve Martin*

How would you act if you felt you were about to be cheated out of millions? Who could you trust? Campbell Scott faces that challenge in David Mamet's brilliant thriller, *The Spanish Prisoner*.

Joe Ross (Scott) has developed a top secret formula for "The Process" that stands to make his company an enormous amount of money. During a trip to the Caribbean to meet with top stockholders, Ross believes his boss, Klein (Ben Gazzarra), may be trying to cut him out of the picture and cheat him out of his fair share. In steps mysterious stranger Jimmy Dell (Steve Martin), who quickly befriends Joe.

**What happens next will amaze you.**

David Mamet has written a classic thriller that challenges your mind. You will regret missing any moment of this movie. Often, I found myself stopping the tape and reviewing it to see what I missed or trying to pick up on small hints. Every move and occurrence, no matter how insignificant, is crucial. More importantly, you don't know whom to trust because no one is who he appears to be. The plot twists will thrill you, and the intelligent script will mesmerize you. As you realize what has happened, you will greatly appreciate the planning that went into laying out such a great storyline.

*The Spanish Prisoner* is a perfect example of the type of movie Hollywood doesn't make any more. It is too intelligent. It makes you think. You can't explain the plot in seven words or less. More importantly, you can't predict what is going to happen.

Unlike most modern movies, this film shocks mentally instead of visually. The audience sees danger approaching which causes your mind to run wild with worry. The audience asks itself, how will Joe get out of this predicament?

Like the great Hitchcock films, Mamet lets the audience scare itself instead of providing a terrifying visual. Mamet also creates a fantastic atmosphere and feel to the movie. It is punctuated with staccato dialogue to keep you on your toes and a bit unsettled. Every actor picks up on this feeling and reflects it in his or her performance.

Campbell Scott is one of the most underappreciated actors in the business. In this movie, he perfectly portrays his character's frustration and fish-out-of-water mentality. Joe Ross is the son of a working class family and unfamiliar with the politics of high stakes business. This only adds to his paranoia and the audience's concern for him.

Steve Martin takes this opportunity to remind us that he can act with the best of them. Because of Martin's slick performance, the audience can understand why Joe trusts this man and seeks his counsel. It is a restrained, but stylish performance. Martin has great dramatic ability. Someday, people will start recognizing this talent is just as great as his comedy.

Mamet and the cast, especially Martin, should have gotten greater kudos. If you want a thriller that makes you think, rent *The Spanish Prisoner*.

# *In Country*

◆

## *Starring Bruce Willis, Emily Lloyd and Joan Allen*

It's very easy to forget why we celebrate Memorial Day. We get so wrapped up in the barbecues, fun at the beach and excitement of having a day off from work and school that the real meaning of the holiday is lost. That's why it's a good idea to watch *In Country* starring Bruce Willis and Emily Lloyd.

Made in 1989, the movie addresses the war America wishes it could forget—Vietnam. As someone who grew up in the eighties, I remember this period of soul searching. The 80's brought a series of movies that addressed these forgotten heroes, including *Platoon*, *Born on the Fourth of July*, *Full Metal Jacket*, *Missing in Action* and *Rambo*. *In Country* was lost among this group, but still holds up well.

Emily Lloyd stars as Sam, a young Kentucky high school graduate. Like every new graduate, she is questioning where her life is going and faces a number of very important decisions regarding her college education and a marriage proposal she received from boyfriend, Lonnie. Sam also is questioning her past.

Her father died in Vietnam before she was born. Her mother (Joan Allen) has left behind all memories of her life with Sam's father, remarried, had another child and moved away to Lexington. She even leaves Sam behind. However, Sam has always wondered what her father was like, why he died and what he died for.

One day, she finds a series of letters written by her father when he was in Vietnam; what veterans refer to as "in country". She reads these letters in an attempt to learn about the father she never met. She also wants to learn about her Uncle Emmett.

Emmett, played by Bruce Willis, is a Vietnam veteran haunted by his experiences. He still has flashbacks of different battles and suffers from other unspecified physical ailments that he refuses to see a doctor about. Like his group of Vietnam veteran buddies, he resents never being honored for service to his country like veterans in wars before them. He lives a simple life trying to deal with his pain. Sam persistently attempts to force him to explain what happened in Vietnam, but he refuses because it brings up too many memories that she could never understand.

Sam's quest becomes complicated when she is given a series of diaries written by her father. She is suddenly faced with the truth about Vietnam.

> **Like millions of Americans, can she face that truth and still respect her father, Uncle Emmett and his buddies?**

Rent *In Country* for two reasons. First, you need to be reminded that Bruce Willis can act. While most of us remember him for his TV sensation *Moonlighting* and the *Die Hard* movies (and want to forget him for dreadful fare like *Hudson Hawk*), he is a talented actor. Willis has always done a fantastic job of balancing big blockbusters with smaller fare like *In Country* and future *WaffleMovies.com* selection *Nobody's Fool*.

It is refreshing to see the bluster Willis shows as a leading man disappear when he takes smaller challenging roles such as this. Someday, a role like this could lead to more recognition of his immense acting ability.

In this movie, Willis deftly portrays a man slightly on the edge, but sane enough to realize that he is troubled. He shows the frustration his character feels with his mental anguish and the sorrow he feels because he came back when many of his friends did not.

The second reason to rent *In Country* is the powerful closing scene at the Vietnam Veterans Memorial in Washington, DC. You must remember that the memorial was in its infancy when this movie was made and many were only starting to learn about it. Willis steals the show as Emmett finds the names of his fallen comrades and finally faces his experiences in Vietnam.

If you are a fan of Bruce Willis or want a better understanding of the pain felt by Vietnam veterans, rent it tonight.

# *Shout*

## *Starring John Travolta, James Walters, Heather Graham and Gwyneth Paltrow*

You would think that a movie starring John Travolta, Heather Graham and Gwyneth Paltrow would be a huge blockbuster. However, if that movie was made in 1991 before Heather and Gwyneth were stars and Travolta was in the midst of career recovery, no one has heard of it, until now.

*Shout*, set in the early 1950's, stars James Walters as Jesse Tucker, a trouble-making orphan who has run afoul of the law one too many times. He is sent to live at the Benedict Boys Home, a half way house for troubled teen boys in the middle of the Texas plains. Jesse has a bad attitude and disrespect for authority, just the kind of boy Benedict (Richard Jordan) wants to break (and women just love to fall for).

The Benedict Boys Home also has a band that plays every July 4th at the town fair, so Benedict hires a new music teacher, the mysterious Jack Cabe (John Travolta). Cabe has an unorthodox teaching method, a love for music and a clouded past. In many ways, Jesse and Cabe are kindred spirits who soon earn each other's respect and admiration.

Things seem to be going along smoothly until the guys in the band hear a new kind of music coming from Cabe's cabin. It stirs their emotions and gives them new hope. It is rock and roll. The boys want to learn how to play this music, but Cabe is reluctant. He makes a deal with them. He will teach them rock and roll if they learn their music for the July 4th celebration.

It's not a movie about rebellion unless we have two star crossed lovers. In *Shout*, Sara (Heather Graham), Benedict's cherished daughter, catches the eye of all the boys. However, it's Jesse who is the most interested. He makes a bet with the other guys. He tells them he will "score" with Sara before the end of the summer, but his plan gets complicated when the two young kids fall in love and his conscience starts to take over.

### *What is Cabe running from?*

### *Will Jesse and Sara be able to fall in love without Benedict breaking them up?*

### *What will Benedict do when he finds out that Cabe is teaching rock and roll to the boys?*

You have to love a movie where John Travolta sings and dances. That gets the movie up to B+ status right away. The role isn't too challenging for Travolta, but he does a great a job. Yes, Travolta's role is very similar to Robin Williams in *Dead Poets Society*, but that's OK. He is able to convey his character's love for music and caring for the trouble teens.

James Walters is actually good in this role. Many of you probably remember him from FOX's manufactured rock band/television show, *The Heights*, or his appearances on *Beverly Hills 90210*, so you already know he can sing. Walters does a good job of showing some depth to the character. He could have easily been an angry, rebel without a clue, but Walters is able to show that Jesse is just as vulnerable as everyone else and looking for something to believe in.

Heather Graham puts in a solid performance, but the role doesn't give her much of a challenge. She was just getting her career underway. *Shout* was made after her stunning appearance in *Drugstore Cowboy* and before her strong turn *in Six Degrees of Separation*. If you are a big fan, you'll want to check this one out just to say you have seen every Heather Graham movie.

I can hear everyone shouting at this review, "What about Gwyneth?" She plays the small role of Rebecca, the object of Allen's (Glenn Quinn) affection. Gwyneth doesn't get much to do, but it was a surprise to see her in this film. By the way, her hair is not blonde in this film. Does that mean that Hollywood starlets don't achieve their looks through natural means?

Kudos to Director Jeffrey Hornaday and the cinematographer for some fantastic sweeping scenes of the Texas plains. The shots give you an understanding of how far away from civilization the home is located and a sense of their isolation.

Take a chance and rent *Shout*.

# Welcome to Sarajevo

✦

## Starring Woody Harrelson, Stephen Dillane and Marisa Tomei

Set in 1992 Sarajevo, and based on actual events, this picture examines the human and societal casualties of war. The picture opens with a family escorting their young bride to her wedding. As they make their way down the street, a sniper shoots the mother of the bride. Yet another reminder that daily life in war torn Sarajevo can never escape the horror of war.

In this scene, we meet Joe Flynn (Woody Harrelson), an American reporter who stops reporting to help a priest carry the mortally wounded mother into a church. Joe is cocky, but also good at heart as he continues to carry out kind deeds for people he doesn't even know.

His fellow reporter is the British Michael Henderson (Stephen Dillane). Michael is quickly growing tired of the horror that surrounds him and the world's lack of interest. Henderson is haunted by the memory of an altar boy who witnesses the mother's death as well as a young girl who he finds orphaned in a hospital after a mortar attack on citizens waiting in line for bread. He decides to take action when a United Nations' delegation descends upon the area to declare Yugoslavia the fourteenth most dangerous place on Earth.

Henderson begins a series profiling an orphanage located on the front lines. He finds children of all ages living in fear and taking care of each other with the help of one adult. During his visits, he befriends a pre-teen girl, Emira (Emira Nuseric) who serves as surrogate mother to a baby named Roadrunner. He promises to get Emira out of harm's way if he gets the chance. After the UN delegation leaves the country without rescuing any of the children, Henderson loses hope.

However, his reporting has grabbed the attention of Nina (Marisa Tomei) and her children's aid group that helps to find homes for the Yugoslavian orphans. Unfortunately, only babies are wanted for adoption, so Henderson pledges to take Emira to England instead of letting her be left behind. The group of children, Nina and Henderson depart the front lines on a dangerous escape for Italy.

**Can they complete this dangerous trek through the war torn countryside and avoid hostile troops gathering up people for concentration camps?**

The movie was beautifully and sensitively made. Director Michael Winterbottom and screenwriter Frank Cottrell Boyce vividly express the societal destruction that has occurred. They show the destroyed lives, families that have been split up, and the desolation that everyone attempts to cope with. This is best exemplified by the group of Yugoslavians befriended by Henderson and his producer.

The group of twenty-somethings reside in a bombed out bar without life's simplest pleasures and amenities. One of them is an accomplished musician who spends his days playing the piano and promising to play a concert when Sarajevo is declared the most dangerous place on Earth. Like the rest of those deeply effected by the war, this small group tries to survive instead of trying to live.

Winterbottom brilliantly intersplices scenes with actual news footage to give the film the feel of a documentary and keeps the viewer aware that many of these horrors are being carried out thousands of miles away as you sit safely in your living room. The picture is also bolstered by beautiful cinematography that captures the devastation of this city that hosted the 1984 Olympics.

Winterbottom and Boyce also produce a realistic portrayal of the reporters covering the atrocities. We watch them struggle to cover the horror, while trying to remain professionally detached. However, they are human and question the reason behind it all, why no one cares, and how they can get out.

Stephen Dillane is wonderful as Henderson. He portrays the character as an everyman caught in the middle of extraordinary events. Dillane avoids making the character overly heroic and preachy. Henderson realizes that he cannot save the world, but he can help a few. It is a wonderful opportunity for Dillane after he had to suffer through the Denis Leary-Sandra Bullock disaster *Two if by Sea*.

Woody Harrelson continues to prove that he is one of the finest, most versatile actors of his generation. Harrelson plays the cocky celebrity reporter with a heart of gold by allowing the character's caring nature and vulnerability shine through. Harrelson is equally adept at taking on roles as zany leading men (*Cheers, White Men Can't Jump*) as well as excellent supporting roles such as this one. This ability will serve him well and give him a long, successful career if he can just stop all of the off-screen hijinxs.

America's involvement in this struggle came seven years after the events of the movie take place. For those who do not have a full understanding of the history of the conflict, the entire movie—most importantly the opening scenes—provide a history lesson.

# Finding Graceland

✦

## *Starring Harvey Keitel, Jonathan Schaech and Bridget Fonda*

Long live the King? That's the premise of this 1998 drama/comedy starring Harvey Keitel and Jonathan Schaech.

Keitel plays "Elvis", a man who may or may not be the king of rock and roll, Elvis Presley. Elvis claims he his heading home to Graceland, where the anniversary of his "death" is being recognized by thousands of fans. He claims that life just became too much to handle in 1977, so he disappeared to escape all the attention and troubles. After over twenty years on the road, Elvis plans on revealing himself to the fans and restarting his career.

Over the years, he explains that Elvis has spent his time in seclusion helping lost souls. On this journey back to Graceland (located in Memphis, Tennessee), he has stumbled across a man who desperately needs his help. Byron (Jonathan Schaech) lost his wife in a tragic car accident over a year ago, and blames himself for the loss. Since her death, he has dropped out of medical school and wandered aimlessly from place to place, but refusing to ever return to Memphis, the site of the accident. He picks up Elvis and promises to take him towards Tennessee.

Byron is convinced that Elvis, while an amiable fellow, is not the King (since he looks like Harvey Keitel, he is probably right). However, other characters that meet Elvis are made into true believers. Even Byron's curiosity is whetted as Elvis reveals facts about his life that only the real King would know. He also knows too many facts about the death of Byron's wife.

### *Can Elvis find his way towards Graceland?*

### *Will Byron forgive himself for his wife's death?*

### *Is this really Elvis?*

Keitel is not believable as Elvis, but that is the point and charm of this movie. He doesn't look like him. He doesn't sound like him. Yet, the audience is slowly drawn in as Elvis credibly recites facts and stories that only he could. Keitel plays the role well by not going over the top and being unbelievable enough to make the audience wonder. That's a difficult task for an actor, and certainly opened himself up to unfair criticism that he wasn't a good impersonator, but Keitel pulls it off perfectly. You'll want to make sure that you catch Elvis attempting his big comeback with the celebrity impersonators. Is he really Elvis? You have to watch the movie to find out.

Schaech and co-star Bridget Fonda are just along for the ride. Schaech is fine as the disbelieving Byron, but I never felt like he had any chemistry with Keitel. Fonda is better and does a great Marilyn Monroe impression. As her character says, it's all in the hair and makeup.

The movie was written and directed by David Winkler, the son of long time *Happy Days* star, Henry Winkler. After receiving the support of the Presley Estate, Winkler was the first director allowed to film in the actual Graceland mansion. Priscilla Presley, Elvis's ex-wife and the executive producer of the film, said she was happy to support the project. She told *USA Today*, "When I read the script for *The Road to Graceland* (the original title of the film), it was so unique and uplifting, and it captured how deeply and personally Elvis—his life and work—can affect people's lives. That's what was really meaningful for me, and why I got involved and brought the management team in to support it."

Overall, this is a great movie for fans and non-fans alike.

# *Election*

### *Starring Reese Witherspoon and Matthew Broderick*

I remember how my High School presidential election was always a popularity contest, which is probably why I didn't win (politics taught me to blame the process if you don't win). Usually the quarterback or cheerleader won and the student government didn't do anything to change or enhance our high school experience, which suited everyone just fine. They got something to put on their transcripts in an attempt to go to a better college and our lives rolled along without any additional hassle.

In many ways, it is just like the elections we hold every year for Mayor, Congress and President. We choose between the lesser of two evils and the results rarely effect our everyday lives. However, to those involved, the election is a life or death monumental event. *Election* effectively portrays the big presidential race as seen through the eyes of the combatants to produce a hilarious farce that can be enjoyed by all.

Jim McCallister (Matthew Broderick) is a popular and successful teacher for a small high school in Omaha, Nebraska. He has been teaching for twelve years and awarded Teacher of the Year three times. McAllister loves his job, working with the students and the quiet life he has made with his wife, but things start to unravel when his best friend and colleague, Dave loses his job after carrying on an affair with a student. McAllister is feeling pressure from his wife to get pregnant, he is helping Dave's wife get over the trauma of her husband's infidelity and he is dreading this year's student government election because it will put him in constant contact with the school's version of Nixon, Tracy Flick (Reese Witherspoon)

Flick is the ultimate overachiever. She is in every club, student government committee and theater production. Tracy is obsessed with success, but, outside of accolades and awards, doesn't know how to measure it. She doesn't feel the other students appreciate what she has done for them, which leads to a lonely life, but continues her crusade. Now, Flick feels it is her destiny to become Student Government President. McAllister, the student government advisor, dreads the idea of working with this annoying, overbearing, psychotic, obsessively ambitious brat, so he decides to teach her a lesson by encouraging the school's popular, star quarterback, Paul (Chris Klein) to run against her.

***Will Tracy be able to defeat Paul in this battle of the titans?***

That may seem like a pretty simple story, but writer/director Alexander Payne has developed a much more layered and complicated film which borders on brilliance. Payne does a great job letting each of the characters deliver voiceover monologues that reveal their true intentions and feelings. We learn about Tracy's jealousy towards Paul and how she feels he has an easy life because he is rich and popular. We hear about the secret grudge McAllister holds against Tracy. We learn that Paul is the one character pure of heart, but dumb as stone. Payne also does a wonderful job of creating a complex world for McAllister, so we understand why he has reached the breaking point and why he blames Tracy for most of it. I have intentionally tried to hold back as much information as possible, because the twists and turns are very enjoyable for the viewer.

Reese Witherspoon is excellent as Tracy Flick. She really camps it up and takes the character to the extreme. In many ways, she is the Stepford high school senior. Witherspoon is able to portray the character's ambition in a very comedic light, but also get sympathy from the audience. Haven't we all worked very hard for a promotion or award only to have it swiped away by someone with the right family ties or other unfair advantage? She is able to show the character's loneliness and desperate attempts to live up to her mother's unfair expectations. She is also downright hilarious.

Matthew Broderick is fantastic as the teacher who has just had enough. Although his life is very good, his character seems to want something more, but can't define what he is missing. This leads the character to make some horrible mistakes in an effort to find a happiness he can't define. Broderick has great timing and the ability to express his character's feelings facially. He also does a great job with physical comedy.

The surprise performance of the film belongs to Chris Klein, his debut after being discovered by Payne while scouting locations. Instead of falling into the stereotypical role of dumb jock, he makes his character the one good person in the film. He is pure of heart, truly cares about his sister and Tracy, and rides life's twists and turns much like Forrest Gump.

Payne grew up in Omaha, so he felt it would be a perfect setting for his second film. While scouting locations and finding extras, he made Witherspoon go undercover as a transfer student for two weeks to see how kids in High School behaved. Having spent most of her life in front of the camera, she never had a true High School experience, so Payne wanted the young actress to learn what it was like. The experiment paid off when Witherspoon's guide turned out to be divine inspiration for the character of Tracy Flick.

For a hilarious evening, rent *Election*.

# *American Buffalo*

◆

## *Starring Dennis Franz and Dustin Hoffman*

It isn't often that a great play is made into a fantastic movie. However, the big screen production of David Mamet's classic, *American Buffalo*, is a fine film that never received the acclaim it deserves.

Dennis Franz stars as a junk shop owner named Donny. He feels a coin collector swindled him by purchasing a rare, valuable Buffalo head nickel for much less than it was worth. Even though he made a nice profit, Donny harbors resentment and embarrassment that he didn't know the true value of the prize, so he plans on breaking into the collector's house to steal it back.

He can't pull off the caper by himself, so he enlists the aid of a young boy, Bobby (Sean Nelson). Bobby and Donny share a father/son relationship, so the young man wants to help him in return for all of the aid and instruction Donny has provided. However, Bobby is very young. Donny feels guilty for getting him involved in an illegal act and doesn't feel the kid is up to the task.

Sensing opportunity, Teach (Dustin Hoffman) interjects himself into the plan, quickly becomes the ringleader and cuts Bobby out in the process. Teach feels he has the ability to pull of the robbery and wants to prove his worth to Donny. Donny doesn't have much faith in Teach, so he also enlists the aid of Fletcher, a man Teach envies.

Greed quickly consumes the group. As the pressure mounts and things start to go awry, Donny learns the truth about his rag-tag gang.

### *Can they pull off the job?*

Dustin Hoffman puts in the best performance. The opening scene where he rants about supposed mistreatment at the diner is classic. It reveals everything we need to know about the character; his feelings of inadequacy, his desire to be an "important" man, and the anger against the world that he harbors just below the surface. You'll be amazed at the amount of dialogue he deftly performs. Watch Hoffman as Teach constantly tries to prove his intelligence. He is also fantastic as Teach slowly becomes consumed with paranoia and his feeling that Donny does not appreciate his friendship.

The other performances are well done, but don't reach Hoffman's level. Dennis Franz is a little too reminiscent of his television character, Andy Sipowitz of *NYPD Blue*. He might have benefited by playing the character with a different accent or some physical uniqueness. However, there are other moments when he shines, particularly scenes with Sean Nelson. In these scenes, Franz displays a mentor/fatherly attitude towards the young boy and expresses a wonderful tenderness. Director Michael Corrente admits that he didn't use Franz the way he should have, so I'll blame him.

Sean Nelson also delivers a spotty performance. He is fantastic in the opening scenes as the eager youth trying to please a man he admires, but isn't as believable towards the end of the movie when his actions are being questioned by Teach.

Mamet's script is the most important ingredient in this three actor, one set film. Many consider the theater version of *American Buffalo* to be Mamet's greatest work, even eclipsing his Pulitzer Prize winning *Glengarry Glen Ross*. The script delivers a solid character study of two losers trying to prove their importance and one kid trying to prove his manhood.

The entire picture was shot in Pawtucket, RI. Director Corrente is a local boy who also filmed his first feature, *Federal Hill*, in the state. Corrente and crew shot the film in just 28 days, paying all of the actors union approved scale for their work, only $2,047 per week as opposed to the millions Franz and Hoffman can command.

The casting of Hoffman proved to be an interesting story. Originally slated to star in the film were Robert DeNiro, Al Pacino and Leonardo DiCaprio, but the casting didn't work out. Pacino played the role to great acclaim on Broadway and was always the first choice to be Teach. However, fate usually leads to Pacino and Corrente butting heads over *American Buffalo*.

In the early eighties, Corrente was staging a production of the play in Boston. Just three days before the start of the run, Pacino's agency called Corrente and informed him that his rights to the play had been rescinded. Pacino was going to do a national tour of the play and Boston was chosen as the first city.

Pacino was Corrente's first choice for the film version, but when he passed on the film project, Corrente tracked down Hoffman and completed the deal in just one afternoon. Before you start thinking ill of Mr. Pacino, you should know that any bad blood between him and the director has been forgotten. Pacino attended the premiere of the film and praised it.

Hoffman turned in a fantastic performance and went the extra step. Even though he was the second choice, Hoffman made the project his number one priority. Not only did he take a greatly reduced salary, Hoffman became involved in the editing process. After seeing a first cut, he praised Corrente, but had some suggestions, and became part of the editing process by sitting with Corrente in the editing bay and reviewing everything.

Hoffman, Franz and Nelson also amazed the community with their generosity. During filming, the three actors gave a special benefit reading of the play, which raised $15,000 for the Trinity Repertory Company. Even the air conditioner from Hoffman's trailer was given to a local theater.

If you're a big Dustin Hoffman fan, check out *American Buffalo*.

# *Two Bits*

◆

## *Starring Al Pacino, Jerry Barone and Mary Elizabeth Mastrantonio*

We are all familiar with Al Pacino's ability to express the rage and anger his character harbors. Some of his greatest work consists of dramatic, explosive scenes in *And Justice for All*, *Dog Day Afternoon*, *The Godfather* and *The Insider*. In *Two Bits*, Pacino shows an ability to play a subtle and quiet character, so turn the volume back up so you can hear him.

The movie focuses on 12-year old Gennaro (Jerry Barone). Growing up in South Philadelphia during the Great Depression, a young boy like Gennaro must find creative ways to entertain himself, since the family has very little money.

Gennaro spends most days in the backyard with his dying Grandfather (Al Pacino). Grandpa dispenses sage advice and stories of the old days to entertain, educate and, sometimes, annoy the young boy. Grandpa knows he has very few days left on this earth, so he promises to give Gennaro his only possession, a quarter, on the day he passes. Years later, even Gennaro looks back and realizes that, "only a dumb kid would make such a deal."

One particularly hot summer day, Gennaro is excited about the opening of a new theater, La Paloma. The theater promises a chance to, "get out of the heat, get out of the Depression" by spending two hours in air conditioning and plush seats, while watching an entertaining film. Gennaro desperately wishes to go to the opening, but does not have the required admission of twenty-five cents. Grandpa teases him and tells him that today might be the day he finally gets the quarter, but Gennaro wants to earn the money a different way. As the day progresses and Gennaro tries to earn the twenty-five cents at various odd jobs, he learns some hard lessons in life, desperation and the depression all around him.

*What is in store for Gennaro?*

While Pacino is a commanding figure in the film and the person most will rent the movie to see, he is not the star. Director James Foley knew he had to select a smart and tough kid to play opposite Pacino. The film would suffer if the actor was intimidated by Pacino. After a nation wide search, where he interviewed over 730 young actors, Foley found Barone. It was a good choice.

The young thespian is in every scene of the 90-minute film and doesn't disappoint. Like most 12-year old kids, he doesn't understand what is going on around him and has no concept of death or poverty. Some critics felt his lack of reaction to very emotional scenes in the film displayed a lack of talent, but I feel it was very realistic. Let's not give kids too much credit. Most young children are not and should not be so emotionally mature. Kids are able to brush off horrible incidents because they don't have an understanding of the weight of what has happened. Barone and screenwriter Joseph Stefano capture that as Gennaro witnesses some very intense scenes.

In many ways, his grandfather encourages this behavior by Gennaro. In one of the later and best scenes, Grandpa gives his most important advice to Gennaro. He tells him to always, "want." He is trying to tell his grandchild to stay young for as long as possible and always strive for bigger and better even though the odds are against it. It is a beautiful scene from Pacino.

Of course, Pacino is fantastic in this film. He is able to show the need for redemption that each of us needs on our deathbed. His character is desperately trying to find inner peace by correcting the wrongs in his life, educating and preparing his grandson for the future and making the end less painful for his daughters. In many ways, the film is a 90-minute long death scene for Pacino, but he does it well.

Surprisingly, the same man who brought you the Alfred Hitchcock classic *Psycho* wrote this film. Written in 1970 by Joseph Stefano, *Two Bits* is an autobiographical tale about one crucial day in his life, while he was a boy in South Philadelphia during the Depression. It was one of only seven of his scripts that were produced for the big screen.

Unfortunately, the film came out a few weeks before Pacino's 1995 blockbuster, *Heat*. Because Pacino was busy hyping *Heat*, the film made very little money and was not widely distributed.

# *Mad City*

◆

## *Starring John Travolta and Dustin Hoffman*

At *Wafflemovies.com*, I often review small, independent movies that weren't blessed with the strong studio backing Universal, Warner Brothers, or Disney can offer. However, you can't call a movie starring John Travolta and Dustin Hoffman a small indie flick. *Mad City* falls into another category of Back Shelf Beauties, movies that were overhyped and couldn't live up to unfairly high expectations.

*Mad City* tackles a subject most Americans have become fascinated with, but also loathe; the media. Specifically, the movie addresses how the media drives the story rather than reports the news. Writer Tom Matthews and director Constantin Costas-Gavras examine the modern media, its drive to get the story at any costs, how regular people broker temporary media celebrity into careers, how celebrity changes their personality, the modern day lack of journalistic integrity, competition between news outlets and sacrifice of the truth for the sake of the story.

At the center of the story is Max Bracket. Dustin Hoffman brilliantly portrays this former network correspondent who has been reduced to working for a local affiliate in Madeline, California due to an ugly on-air dispute with the anchor of the evening news. Bracket desperately wants to escape Madeline and return to his former glory. Opportunity knocks when he is locked in the local natural history museum men's room as former security guard Sam Bailey (John Travolta) holds the curator and a dozen children hostage.

*Will Bracket get the big story, or get hurt?*

Bracket represents a belief that is prevalent among most journalists. I call it the Bob Woodward-syndrome. Those afflicted with the syndrome believe they can become major media celebrities by catching a break and covering one big story like Woodward and Bernstein did with the Watergate scandal. Hoffman is experienced with this type of reporter since he played Bernstein in *All the President's Men*, so he puts in a strong performance as Bracket senses his opportunity to befriend the slow-witted Sam and seize control of the situation.

Like many thrust into the media spotlight, Sam Bailey becomes a pawn of the media. Although he is a pawn, he also becomes taken with the chance to be a celebrity. Bracket spins Sam's story as successfully as the highest paid public relations consultant. Within hours, Sam has gone from being a felon to a loved and sympathetic public figure. Bracket tells Sam he could have his own fishing show, TV movie and book deal. He clearly does not have Sam's interest in mind. Bracket's eye is on a bigger prize, the chance to cover the story for the network.

Travolta does a commendable job of portraying Bailey as a sympathetic character. He is a former member of the Air Force who couldn't realize his goal of becoming a pilot due to the lack of a college education. He is a loving husband and father who can't summon up the courage to tell his wife, Jenny (Lucinda Jenny), that he has lost his job due to budget cuts, so he dresses for work everyday and goes to the movies.

Travolta is at his best when he plays the character as sympathetic and vulnerable. He does a wonderful job in the movie's closing scenes as Sam becomes desperate. However, his performance suffers when he tries to portray rage and madness. Sam Bailey is reminiscent of Michael Douglas' character in *Falling Down*; however, he just isn't believable when the character is outraged. This can be blamed equally on Travolta, who tries to reprise part of his character in *White Man's Burden*, and Mathews, who doesn't establish enough motivation for the character's outrage. His situation is believable, but the character is more of a dumb lug than a homicidal maniac.

The movie is blessed with a powerful supporting cast. Many of you will recognize Alan Alda playing CTN network news anchor Kevin Hollander. Hollander has a nose for the story and sees an opportunity to steal glory from Bracket, the man who embarrassed him on the air. Robert Prosky plays Lou Potts, news director for KXBD-Madeline. Potts is a news veteran who becomes disgusted with the entertainment program the evening news has become. Lucinda Jenny puts in a strong performance as Sam's loving wife and Ted Levine distinguishes himself as police Chief Alvin Lemke.

Mia Kirshner stands out as Laurie, an intern with stars in her eyes. She starts the movie as a naïve kid who helps a downed security guard rather than filming the action after he is shot. She learns her first lesson when Bracket tells her, "make a decision if you are going to be a part of the story or whether you are going to be there to record the story." Laurie quickly sees that her opportunity for stardom also has arrived, and she attacks the chance as ferociously as Bracket or Hollander. Like other journalists, she has fallen victim to the Woodward-syndrome.

The movie does a good job of describing the power of television and how it seduces Laurie, Sam and Bracket. It shows how regular everyday citizens become celebrities simply by appearing on television. People who don't know Sam are interviewed as his friends. His true friends sell their stories to tabloid news programs. Other players in the situation realize how they can benefit from the exposure they have received. Even the FBI engages in reverse spin by portraying Sam as a crazed lunatic who should be brought to justice by any means necessary.

Certainly, members of the media do not do a good job of defending their profession. Writer Mathews should be commended for avoiding the sanctimonious feel that many Hollywood interpretations of the modern media often take on. However, the movie drags in the middle, so I advise anyone who rents the movie to have faith. The movie has a strong climax and is a good rental.

# The Hudsucker Proxy

❖

## Starring Tim Robbins, Paul Newman and Jennifer Jason Leigh

This film is a great example of why I love movies. Nothing excites me as much as a brilliant movie with an interesting plot, fantastic acting, wild visuals and a strong script. This one has it all, and then some.

In this movie, Hudsucker Industries is facing a great crisis. The founder and president of the company, Waring Hudsucker (Charles Durning), has passed away without leaving a will. According to law, his 87% of the company must be made available on January 1, 1959 in a public stock offering. This turn of events has devastated the Board of Directors, who fear an outsider will purchase the company and toss them out of their positions of power and wealth. However, Sydney Mussburger (Paul Newman), has a plan.

Sydney, Hudsucker's #2, thinks this is a great opportunity to make some money and gain control of the presidency that Waring would never give him. He proposes that the board sell its stock, appoint an utter boob to the presidency, let him drive down the stock price through mismanagement and incompetence, then buy a controlling share of Hudsucker on January 1 when no one else will want to touch the stock. After assuming control of the company, Sydney will be installed as president and resurrect the business. To make the plan work, he must find a complete and utter idiot to ruin the company.

Fresh off the bus from the Muncie College of Business Administration, Norville Barnes (Tim Robbins) needs a job. He goes to the unemployment office, but realizes he is unqualified for most jobs, except an opening in the Hudsucker Industries mailroom. It's not the best job in the world, but Norville has big ideas about a new product for kids that will propel him up the ladder of success. Unfortunately, he is a nervous klutz who almost kills Sydney Mussburger during his first day on the job. Yes, Sydney has found his imbecile.

**Can Norville succeed as president of Hudsucker Industries?**

**Will Sydney's plan be exposed?**

Along with *Raising Arizona* and *Fargo*, *The Hudsucker Proxy* is another example Joel and Ethan Coen's brilliance. What seems like a complicated plot is easily laid out and performed to perfection thanks to a fantastic screenplay written in the style of a '30's-era screwball comedy. Joel Coen, who serves as director, is able to put together some fantastic sequences ranging from Robbins' first scenes at the employment office to flashback scenes to a mailroom that appears to be taken straight out of a pro-Marxist German film to production and marketing of a new Hudsucker product. Coen's directing teamed with some wonderfully done art direction and set creation places the film above and beyond most films you will ever see. Every line, every costume, every set is designed to create an overall indictment of the corporate world.

Tim Robbins is hilarious as the naïve, innocent, hard working imbecile who has been given the opportunity of a lifetime. We all know he has great comedic timing and ability, but he showcases some amazing physical comedy ability. Also, the teaming of Robbins with Jennifer Jason Leigh, a reporter who secretly goes undercover to seek out the truth about Norville, is extraordinary. Leigh's dead-on performance as a "fast talking career gal" is reminiscent of Katherine Hepburn at her finest. She understands how to use the rhythm of her dialogue to bring the character to life. The two play out their romantic pairing with an energy that keeps it from becoming corny.

They don't make movies like *The Hudsucker Proxy* anymore. Every actor understands his role and gives a memorable performance. Plus, each scene has layers of intrigue and humor that contribute to the overall enjoyment of the film.

Do yourself a favor and rent *The Hudsucker Proxy*.

*The Classics*

# *The Desperate Hours*

*Starring Humphrey Bogart and Frederic March*

Another mission of this book is to highlight great movies from the past. Some of the greatest films of all time are available on video for you to enjoy. This is one of them.

Humphry Bogart is a legend, but doesn't fit the mold of a matinee idol. He played darker, more mysterious roles than his contemporaries. He paved the way for the antihero roles that made James Dean, Marlon Brando, Al Pacino and Robert DeNiro famous. While Cary Grant and Errol Flynn were playing the shining hero, Bogart was willing to play the bad guy or the moody good guy with a dark side. This is most evident in one of his final and best films, *The Desperate Hours*, which is based on a true story.

Bogart plays Glenn Griffin, a dangerous convict jailed for killing a cop during a violent shootout. Glenn, his brother Hal and another prisoner escape from jail by severely injuring a guard. They need to meet up with an accomplice, who has their getaway money, so they decide to sneak into a small suburb of Indianapolis.

The convicts takeover the Hilliard household and hold husband Dan (Frederic March), wife Ally (Martha Scott), 19-year old Cindy (Mary Murphy) and 7-year old Ralph hostage. Glenn warns them that he will kill the family if the police show up or they decide to try anything funny. Glenn's girlfriend is scheduled to arrive at midnight with their getaway money, so he wants no trouble until then. Although he is angry and wants to protect his family, Dan decides it is best to go along with their captor's demands even though it is a great sacrifice to his pride and manhood.

The three captors have little trust in each other and start disputing the plan, so, when Dan sees this opening, the family decides to fight back.

### *Can they safely escape the ordeal?*

Some of the best films play on our real fears. When this movie came out in the 50's, people were flocking to the suburbs seeking tranquility, privacy and safety that city living could not provide. This movie pierces through that belief to show that danger can reach you anywhere. This situation manifested every suburbanite's deepest fears of having their family in danger and criminals going through their personal belongings and financial records.

Bogart could have easily dominated the film, but smartly plays his role while letting other actors shine. Even though Bogart was almost 60 years old when this movie came out, he still is intimidating and strikes fear in the audience. You don't want to meet up with this guy in a dark alley. His character seems in control, but is consumed with a rage and bitterness that Bogart reveals in small, but effective doses. Watch Bogart's eyes light up to show how much his character enjoys violence.

Bogart and March play a great mental chess game and have good chemistry. You can see each character trying to figure out the other's next move. Bogart brilliantly mocks his opponents thinking process. March is able to evolve his character from a mannered, suburban father into a savage defending his turf. He becomes just as dangerous and cunning as the captors, and makes the audience wonder how far they could go to defend their family.

Another great aspect of the film is the camera work. Since the film is in black and white, the cinematographer is able to effectively use shadows to create an eerie feeling. Try watching the movie with the lights off.

Some of you may remember the remake of this movie, *1990's The Desperate Hours* starring Mickey Rourke, Anthony Hopkins and Mimi Rogers. The remake pales in comparison to the original. Do yourself a favor and rent the classic.

# *It Happened One Night*

## *Starring Clark Gable and Claudette Colbert*

It is one of the most honored films in Hollywood history. It combined some of the biggest talents of the day, before they were huge stars. It even threatened the existence of an entire industry. *It Happened One Night* is one of the best films of all time, and the first to sweep all five major Oscar categories.

The film was named Best Picture of 1934 and led to Academy Awards for Clark Gable, Claudette Colbert, Director Frank Capra and Screenwriter Robert Riskin. Since the movie was such a masterpiece, why was Gable dead set against being involved in the film that defined his career?

Colbert plays Ellie, an heiress with an independent streak. Against her father's (Walter Connelly) wishes, and most likely just to upset him, Ellie secretly elopes with a King. Once she informs her father of the clandestine wedding, he becomes furious and immediately begins to seek an annulment of the marriage. Ellie is tired of her father's domineering ways, so she jumps ship, literally. She dives off their yacht in Miami to make her way to New York to see the King.

Gable plays Peter, a washed up, alcoholic reporter who constantly bickers with his editor. When a drunk Peter goes too far in one of their arguments, the editor fires him leaving Peter stranded in Miami. He buys a bus ticket for New York and settles in for a long, quiet ride. As fate would have it, Ellie has bought a ticket on the same bus and ends up sitting with Peter.

He quickly learns who she is and about the frantic search being mounted for Ellie by the press and her father. Peter realizes that he could have the biggest story of his career and agrees to help her get to New York in exchange for an exclusive. As everything starts to go wrong in their quest to reach New York, the two find themselves falling in love. However, Peter is reluctant to act on his feelings because Ellie is a married woman.

### Can they find true love?

*It Happened One Night* almost didn't happen. After struggling to make it in Hollywood, Gable was starting to come into is own during the early part of the 30's. He had signed a contract with MGM, and was one of their consistent moneymakers. In 1934, legendary MGM chief Louis B. Mayer decided to loan Gable out to Columbia for *It Happened One Night*, which was considered a minor project at the time. Gable was furious. He didn't want to be loaned out to a lesser studio, didn't want to be working on a minor project, and didn't want to share billing with Colbert who was also starting to emerge as a star. Colbert was also upset about the arrangement for similar reasons.

Adding to the stars' discontent was director Frank Capra. At the time, he was considered a second rate director who showed some flashes of talent, but was better known for the Claudette Colbert starring flop, 1927's *For the Love of Mike*. Studios had much more control in those days, so the stars were forced to make the movie. The rest, as they say, is Hollywood history as *It Happened One Night* became an acclaimed film that propelled Columbia to major studio status and elevated Capra to the top tier of directors.

The movie contains some historical Hollywood scenes that have been mimicked many times over, proving its continuing impact on modern movie making. Two scenes will jump out at you immediately. First, Claudette Colbert shows a little leg to succeed at hitchhiking. The other is when Gable puts a sheet over a strung out piece of rope to erect the walls of Jericho and separate the room into two halves. *It*

*Happened One Night* set the standard for romantic and screwball comedies. The film created many gags and elements that are still used in film.

Most movies from the past seem a little slower paced compared to what we are accustomed to today, but this film is remarkably paced as if made in the last few years. Do yourself a favor and rent one of America's finest films.

# A Patch of Blue

◆

## Starring Sydney Poitier, Shelley Winters and Elizabeth Hartman

Sidney Poitier is one of America's greatest actors. He has starred in memorable movies like *Guess Who's Coming to Dinner*, *In the Heat of the Night* and *To Sir with Love*. However, most fans don't know about one of his best movies, *1965's A Patch of Blue*.

Young Selina (Elizabeth Hartman) is an 18-year old blind woman who leads a solitary, lonely, painful life. She is treated like a servant by her mother, Roseanne (Shelley Winters) and her drunken grandfather, Old Pa (Wallace Ford). She yearns to get out of the house and go to the park where she can at least listen to the birds and feel the warmth of the sun. Selina finally gets her wish and meets a young man, Gordon (Sidney Poitier), at the park who treats her with kindness.

Gordon quickly realizes that Selina hasn't acquired any of the skills a blind person needs to be independent. She can't read Braille and doesn't have any ability to get around town. He slowly learns that Selina has a horrible life, so he wants to make it better by teaching her some the skills she needs and enrolling her in a school for the blind.

Along the way, Selina and Gordon start to have feelings for each other. However, Gordon feels the relationship is doomed because he is African-American. He sees the way people look at the two of them when they are together and even faces resistance from his own brother. When he hears about Selina's past relations with African-Americans, he fears that he will lose her if he ever tells her the truth.

### *Can they find happiness?*

The movie benefits from a quartet of fine actors. Poitier is brilliant in this film, and I wish he received an Oscar nomination for his work. His character is heartbreakingly torn between love and what he feels is harsh reality. Poitier especially shines as his character struggles with prejudice on both sides. This film was important for Poitier because he had earned acclaim for his ability, but needed to show bankability (the true measure of an actor by studios, you can be a star even if you stink). As you read on, you'll see if he succeeded.

Elizabeth Hartman makes a strong debut. She poignantly shows her character's immense naivete. Hartman is especially moving when her character starts to realize that her life can be much better, but fears that her family is too much of an obstacle. Hartman went on to star in several other fine films, including Francis Ford Coppola's first studio film, *You're a Big Boy Now*. She was considered one of Hollywood's best and brightest, even garnering an Oscar nomination for this film, a rare feat for a debut performance. However, her career never exploded in the way many predicted, so she left Hollywood, and lived like a recluse in her Manhattan apartment. Eventually, Hartman was overtaken by depression and was admitted to a Pittsburgh psychiatric hospital. In 1987, she was killed in an apparent suicide attempt.

Winters and Ford are fantastic as hopeless, mean, nasty, controlling family members. Winters' character is frighteningly devoid of a conscience for the horrible atrocities she has forced upon her child. She was awarded the Oscar for Best Supporting Actress in 1965 for this role. Ford is remarkably sympathetic as a man with a drinking problem, but also shows a dark side. He does a fine job balancing between the two.

The studio, MGM, felt the picture was very good, but not necessarily a big box office hit. To generate some buzz for the film, MGM distributed it in limited release in the middle of December 1965. This qualified the film for Oscar consideration. After a nomination for Hartman, a win for Winters and other technical awards, the film was released in March of 1966. *A Patch of Blue* went on to become one of the top ten grossing films of 1966, and confirmed Sydney Poitier as a major box office force and talent.

If you are in the mood for a love story, check this one out this weekend. Some scenes are too intense for younger children, but the film would be rated PG-13 under today's system.

# *Marty*

◆

### *Starring Earnest Borgnine*

An Academy Award winner in 1955 for Best Picture, *Marty* is one of the finest films in American history and a timeless classic that inspires all of us to examine our lives and personal motivations. Hiding underneath the saccharine sweet theme song is a powerful look at loneliness, peer pressure and the struggle to find our one true love. Who would have expected something like this from Ernest Borgnine!

Borgnine stars as Marty, a 34-year old, overweight, lonely butcher. All of his brothers and sisters have gotten married, but he feels that it will never happen for him. Marty finally realizes that he's, "tired of looking for a girl every Saturday night of his life." He is tired of the dating scene, rejection and the never ending search for a woman who will look past his appearance to find a kind, caring man.

Marty starts to focus on his future. However, the question of marriage continues to rear its ugly head.

After a heated discussion (one of the best scenes in movie history), his mother (Esther Mincotti) convinces him to go the weekly Saturday night dance at the Stardust Ballroom. When he gets there, Marty meets a female version of himself. Clara (Betsy Blair) is a lonely, shy schoolteacher who is alone in the world, but tired of the rejection she faces when she seeks love.

**Can Marty and Clara overcome their fear of rejection to find love?**

**Are they meant for each other?**

Unfortunately, Ernest Borgnine is not considered to be a fine actor, but this movie earned him an Oscar and gave him the opportunity to show his talent. Borgnine brilliantly portrays the torture Marty goes through just to get up the courage to ask a woman to dance and the rejection of being brushed off. He elicits great compassion and understanding from everyone as he starts to believe that he is not good enough for someone else to love. Watch his painful declaration that, "whatever it is that women want, I ain't got" and his poor self-image.

He also makes wonderfully profound observations about life and love, but hides them under the exterior of an insecure, regular Joe. The character has a grasp of what he wants to say and express, but doesn't have the ability or courage to do so. Borgnine is able to show that his character is a romantic man trapped inside the body and mind of an everyday, average guy, and Delbert Mann deserves kudos for writing such wonderful dialogue.

Mann wrote a fantastic script that captures the hard knocks of single life, the desire for a better life and everyone's battle to choose between someone who is beautiful inside or a trophy boyfriend/girlfriend. The script also captures the desperation and fear of loneliness, the resentment we feel when our friend finds someone special while we sit on the sidelines and the constant challenges to our self-confidence. In a wonderfully layered script, Mann uses Marty and Clara as the main vehicles, but also develops several supporting characters who give us a more complex view of the subject.

One of these characters is Marty's friend, Angie. Instead of being happy that his friend may have found someone special, Angie (Joe Mantell) is driven by jealousy and fear in his attempts to stop Marty from pursuing Clara. Being alone isn't so bad for Angie, as long as he has his friend Marty with him.

Angie also shows the peer pressure we all go through to not only find someone who we care about, but a boyfriend or girlfriend that also serves as some sort of trophy. The boyfriend or girlfriend improves our own self-image as we show the world that we must be someone special if this beautiful person wants to spend time with us.

Marty's mother is also driven by fear of loneliness to interfere in Marty and Clara's relationship. She starts believing that she will become like her sister—a woman passed around from family member to family member like a burden that everyone must bear for a short period of time instead of being the beloved mother and grandmother.

I may never be able to do justice to the film with my writing ability, but I sincerely hope that you will check out *Marty*.

# *A Guy Named Joe*

*Starring Spencer Tracy, Irene Dunn and Van Johnson*

When he remade this film as 1989's *Always*, Steven Spielberg often referred to *A Guy Named Joe* as one of his all-time favorites. With a star-studded lineup and touching story about true love, maybe you will like it too.

Pete Sandidge (Spencer Tracy) and Al Yackey (Ward Bond) are two hot shot Air Force pilots fighting the Axis powers during World War II. Pete drives his commanding officer crazy with daredevil heroic flying to attack enemy targets. Sandidge is good, but he doesn't follow orders and walks around like king of the castle.

Sandidge also dates the prettiest lady in the Air Force, Dorinda Durston (Irene Dunn). She worries about his safety and the damage he is doing to his career. Pete feels he is winning the war, and doesn't care about personal glory or the opinion of his superiors.

When Pete and Al are offered the opportunity to go stateside as training instructors, Dorinda begs Pete to take the offer. If he doesn't take it, she'll leave him. Pete loves Dorinda too much to lose her, so he takes the offer, but his base is suddenly attacked and he dies in a heroic effort to destroy a Nazi war ship.

Pete enters heaven and is chosen to be a guardian angel for pilots. His job is to help and protect Ted Randall (Van Johnson), a rich kid who is too tentative in the cockpit and in life. Pete takes a liking to the young man, and decides to exceed his charge by helping him with his love life and confidence around women. However, trouble arises when Ted meets Dorinda.

### *Can Pete do his job or will he want to keep Ted away from the love of his life?*

Of course, Spencer Tracy is the big star in this film, and he doesn't disappoint. He shows his character's brashness and detest for authority in a way that the audience applauds. I was also taken with Tracy's moving performance as he watched his trainee replace him and take the love of his life away. His reactions are natural and his final course of action leaves the audience awestruck.

Ward Bond puts in a great performance, deftly moving between the comedic and dramatic facets of his character. Irene Dunne does a wonderful job as the independent woman who, while she doesn't go toe to toe with Tracy like Katharine Hepburn could, stands up to Tracy and proves to be a formidable foe.

The other aspect of the movie that I find interesting is the treatment of the war. The movie is ostensibly a war movie, but the war is secondary. Much like in *Casablanca*, the focus is on the characters and the struggles they face, a big departure for the time. The war is simply a backdrop.

If you are in the mood for a good movie, rent *A Guy Named Joe*.

# Angels in the Outfield

## Starring Paul Douglas and Janet Leigh

I was finishing this book as the World Series got underway, and started thinking about the great baseball movies. We're all familiar with *The Natural*, *Field of Dreams*, *Bull Durham* and *The Pride of the Yankees*. However, many of you may have never seen *Angels in the Outfield*. I'm not talking about the Disney remake from a few years ago, but the original family movie made in 1951.

Paul Douglas stars as Guffy McGovern, the foul-mouthed, nasty, gruff manger of the Pittsburgh Pirates. The Pirates are mired in a horrible slump that has taken them to the basement of the National League. They are the laughing stock of the league and the city. The situation has gotten so bad that McGovern has demanded the dismissal of the team's radio announcer, Fred Bayles (Keenan Wynn), for telling the truth.

The Pittsburgh Messenger newspaper has assigned a new reporter to cover the team, Jennifer Page (Janet Leigh), the Household Hints columnist. The editor desperately wants to get a refreshing take on the team and, hopefully, renew interest in the paper's baseball coverage. Well, he gets more than he bargains for in this deal.

Jennifer starts to write scathing columns about the team. She feels the root of all the Pirates' ills lies at the feet of McGovern. If only he started to treat his players better and clean up his act, maybe the team would start to win. One night, as McGovern goes back to the field to find his good luck charm, he discovers that Jennifer's opinion is shared by a higher power.

Someone has been praying to Saint Gabriel, and he has taken a special interest in the case. He sends one of his angels to speak with McGovern. Guffy is told to clean up his act, treat people better, avoid cursing, and stop fighting. In exchange, the angel and his 'Heavenly Choir Nine" will help the Pirates.

To make things difficult, a little girl (Donna Corcoran) sees the angels, the press grabs onto the story and Guffy's mental stability is called into question.

### *Can he keep up his end of the bargain?*

It's fun to sit back and watch such an innocent and charming movie. The child isn't overly precocious and firing off one-liners. McGovern's cursing is distorted so you cannot understand the words, but you know he is swearing. There is even an old-fashioned love story where no one takes off their clothes and has sex on the first date. Living in the 21$^{st}$ century, it is refreshing to find such a clean movie. It is a great choice for the family.

Another aspect of the movie I find interesting is the way it has influenced other modern day movies. McGovern has to turn to the wily veteran pitcher in the twilight of his career (*Major League*) to win the big game. No one, not even religious figures, believe McGovern is actually conversing with celestial beings (*Oh God!*). Rent the movie and see if you can pick out more examples.

All of the stars of the film know their roles and play them well. Paul Douglas is the gruff, but lovable manager with a heart of gold who tries to change his ways. It isn't a challenging role, but Douglas plays both sides of the character well and believably.

Janet Leigh plays McGovern's foil. For the time, her part is very liberated. She is a working woman in her early twenties who isn't afraid to speak her mind. The character does more than bat her eyelashes lovingly at the hero. She challenges him and stands up to him when others are afraid.

Keenan Wynn does a great job as the detestable nemesis who will stop at nothing to destroy the hero. Your home audience will be jeering him. He even scowls well.

If you're in the mood for a good, old-fashioned fun time for the entire family, rent *Angels in the Outfield*. Just make sure you get the 1951 version.

# *Broadcast News*

◆

## *Starring Holly Hunter, William Hurt, Albert Brooks and Jack Nicholson*

During TV sweeps month, you get inundated with programming stunts as networks and their affiliates attempt to raise ratings to determine advertising prices for the coming season. Some of the silliest and most outrageous will be contained in your newscasts. This wasn't the case until a seismic shift 20 years ago in television programming changed how we view news programming and its role.

In my humble opinion, the eighties saw a revolution in the television news business. With the concurrent rise of cable and CNN as well as the increasing corporatization of the networks, news departments were seen as a burden. Traditionally, the networks wanted to have prestigious, first class news organizations, even though they lost money. This attitude changed and these departments were suddenly expected to make a profit, which led to sweeping changes in personnel and content. *Broadcast News* captures this era of change, the hard feelings of traditional newspeople and the negative impact it had on network news as it became entertainment programming hosted by celebrity journalists.

The movie opens with young Tom Grunick asking the innocent, but deadly question, "What can you do with yourself if all you can do is look good?" In the modern world, you can become a network news anchor

The audience is then transported to modern times as Jane (Holly Hunter) and Aaron (Albert Brooks) find themselves tracking down a story in Nebraska. The two have a close friendship with romantic overtones. They also share the view that the news business is going down a dangerous path.

Jane gives a speech to a local broadcasters convention about the evils of news as entertainment and their responsibility to strive for a higher standard, but none of the young, beautiful new wave of broadcasters cares much. They see the future and want to grab on. The only audience member who understands is the grown Tom Grunick (William Hurt).

Tom is guilty over his recent promotion to news anchor because he doesn't feel he earned it and only got the job due to his good looks. He feels he is pretending to be a reporter and doesn't comprehend the news he is reporting. Tom wants to learn how to be a traditional journalist. Then, he drops the bomb. Tom has been hired to work in the Washington bureau of Jane and Aaron's network.

### When the network starts to make budgetary cuts, will Jane, Aaron and Tom lose their jobs?

### When a love triangle develops between the three, who will win Jane's heart?

Writer and Director James L. Brooks created an amazing movie. Even though it was made almost 15 years ago, we are still struggling with many of the same themes of news as entertainment. Brooks also does a wonderful job of creating three central characters who have flaws, but win the love of the audience. Each one suffers from a lack of confidence that is hidden with bravado. They are real people that we can relate to even though you have never worked in a network news bureau.

Unlike most, the love triangle is compelling. Jane is caught between two polar opposites. As a professional newswoman, she has very little respect for Tom, but his good looks and sweetness reel her in. She also has strong feelings for Aaron, her close friend and confidant. The resolution to the story is one you could not expect.

My favorite performer in the movie is Albert Brooks. His character is the nerdy, arrogant smart kid that everyone wanted to beat up in school. He is brilliant, but lacks any sense of modesty and social skill. This attitude hurts Aaron's stellar career and leads many of his co-workers to wish for his failure.

Brooks delivers his lines with great zeal. He seems to revel in being the man everyone hates and envies. His reactions to success and failure are very real, and he should be applauded for this role. Aaron represents the old fashioned, endangered television journalist who sees the future is dim. Brooks could have easily played the role with a straight one-dimensional bitterness, however, he evokes sympathy from the audience because we see his vulnerability, frustration and dreams. We feel for him as he thinks the woman of his dreams is being taken away by a man who represents everything he hates, and he thought she opposed.

I also enjoyed the performance of Holly Hunter as the tough-as-nails female producer struggling to succeed in a male dominated world while also trying to find true love. She represents the struggles every woman faces in the modern world. She brings depth to the character by truly struggling to choose between Tom and Aaron, when the easy choice is to go after the best looking guy.

The movie benefits from great performances from other well-known stars. Jack Nicholson plays network news anchor Bill Rorish like only Jack can, and the movie is worth renting just for Joan Cusack's amazing display of physical comedy in the opening minutes.

# Horse Feathers

### Starring The Marx Brothers

Great comedy comes from great tragedy. When America was swept into the Great Depression and people were living daily dramas that rivaled any movie production, The Marx Brothers burst onto the scene to ridicule convention and take the audience's minds off their troubles.

When Professor Quincy Adams Wagstaff (Groucho Marx) assumes the presidency of Huxley College, he wants to instill pride in the university's students and faculty. His son, Frank (Zeppo Marx), suggests that football is the answer. His father agrees that the university is "neglecting football for education", so the ethically-challenged Professor goes to a speak-easy to hire two local football stars, but Wagstaff's rival, Mr. Jennings (David Landau) of Darwin College, has beaten him to it. Thinking they are the two football stars, Professor Wagstaff accidentally hires Baravelli (Chico Marx) and Pinky (Harpo).

**Is there any way Huxley College can win the big game and save Wagstaff's job?**

As you can imagine, the plot is secondary in most Marx Brothers' movies. Their movies are usually focused on the wild vaudevillian antics of the trio, and there are plenty in this film. Groucho speaks to the audience and cracks stinging one-liners with rapid-fire delivery. Chico plays the piano and causes havoc due to his misunderstanding of the English language. Harpo, as always, is my favorite in this film.

I have always been amazed at Harpo's ability to command the audience's attention with no spoken lines. He tickles your funny bone with crazy antics such as "cutting the cards" with a meat cleaver or giving the password by using props that seem to appear out of thin air. Even more amazing is the change in his demeanor when he begins to the play the harp. Watch how serious he gets when he focuses his energy on making beautiful music.

The Marx Brothers knew their audience. The Brothers ridiculed honored institutions and vented the frustration of millions of poverty stricken Americans. In *Horse Feathers*, they lampoon college sports and the university system at a time when most cannot dream of luxuries such as higher education. Harpo taunts the police when they interfere with his snack break, and even throws in a satire of *Ben Hur*. Chico's struggles with the English language personify the difficulties many had when they came to America, and these fans related to him. The Marx Brothers continued to play on these themes throughout their movie careers.

# *The Mouse That Roared*

*Starring Peter Sellers*

In 1959, America was engaged in an arms race with our main nemesis, the Soviet Union. Much like colonial times, major nations allied with one or the other, often leaving smaller countries out in the cold. Fear about nuclear war was real and many built bomb shelters in case the unimaginable happened. The only way to attack such serious issues in a heated political environment was with humor.

The film opens as the tiny nation of Grand Fenwick decides that action must be taken to secure its future. The 15 ¾ square mile nation in the French Alps has one major export, a fine wine produced by every citizen. America is its number one market, but that market has been seized by a California winery that manufacturers a knock off of the Grand Fenwick brand. This loss of business has caused great panic throughout the nation. The Prime Minister, Count Rupert (Peter Sellers), has logged several protests with the United States, but all have been ignored.

Count Rupert has a plan to save the country from economic ruin. He has noticed that the United States is a very forgiving nation. He wants Grand Fenwick to declare war on the USA, invade New York and surrender immediately (don't let the World Trade Center attacks discourage from watching this film, this is a comedy). After surrender, Count Rupert expects the United States to provide financial aid to rebuild the Grand Fenwick economy, much like it did for other European nations and Japan after World War II. The whole matter should be settled in about 20 minutes. The Parliament and Dutchess Glorianna (Peter Sellers) feel this is an excellent idea, and they have just the man for the job.

Tully Bascom (Peter Sellers) is the head of the military in Grand Fenwick. While the country has been in existence since 1430, the armed forces never evolved. They still wear chainmail suits and use the bow and arrow. Tully is hardly an imposing figure. He gets seasick, isn't very strong, isn't very brave, but that is exactly the type of leader this assignment needs.

Tully and his forces enter the Port of New York looking for someone they can surrender to, but no one is around. President Eisenhower has called for an air raid drill on the East Coast because the US has a new weapon, the Q-bomb. The Q-bomb has been developed by a New York scientist and is more destructive than any other weapon on earth.

Tully reads about the new bomb in the newspaper and gets an idea. He decides to seize the bomb to win the war. When his forces return to Grand Fenwick, they expect a hero's welcome, but the country is very upset that the plan has gone awry. They don't want this kind of power.

**Can Count Rupert, Dutchess Glorianna and Tully find a way to lose the war now that they have won?**

Peter Sellers achieved great acclaim throughout Europe for his ability to play different comedic characters. During the fifties, he was a star on the BBC radio program *The Goon Squad*, which gained him enough popularity to start a career in film. In *The Mouse That Roared*, Sellers shines by creating three distinct and ridiculous characters.

Each character has his or her own quirks. Tully is a meek leader full of fear. The Dutchess wants to do right for her subjects, but is stuck in the 15$^{th}$ century, and Rupert schemes to make himself famous and powerful. Sellers masterfully plays each part to highlight the looniness of each character.

The film marked a distinct departure for director Jack Arnold. Early in his career, Arnold directed and produced about 25 documentaries for government agencies and corporations. He soon moved to Hollywood and made a name for himself directing science fiction and horror films including the genre classics *It Came From Outer Space*, *Creature from the Black Lagoon* and *The Incredible Shrinking Man*.

By presenting its opinions under the shroud of comedy, the film makes a strong statement about nuclear escalation and the treatment of smaller countries by the superpowers. It is a subversive and hilarious film, especially for the time. Check it out this weekend.

# Dr. Jeckyll and Mr. Hyde

❖

## Starring Spencer Tracy, Ingrid Bergman and Lana Turner

Most classic horror films star unknown actors and low cost special effects. However, the 1941 remake of Dr. Jeckyll and Mr. Hyde was driven by the star power and eclectic casting of Spencer Tracy, Lana Turner and Ingrid Bergman.

Set in 1887, Tracy plays the refined, well-known and respected Dr. Jeckyll. Sir Charles, the father of his fiancé, Beatrix (Turner), is pushing Jeckyll to establish a traditional and lucrative medical practice. However, Jeckyll is fascinated with his recent studies of the human mind. He believes each person has a good side and a dark side, which can be controlled with the proper chemicals. Jeckyll feels his studies and experiments will yield medicine to cure metal illness. Although he is discouraged by peers, he forges ahead.

Driven by his desire to prove critics wrong and show his genius, Jeckyll cannot receive approval to test any of his mind-altering drugs on humans, so he decides to use himself as a test subject. He discovers a chemical that unleashes the dark side of man and successfully transforms into an alter ego, Mr. Hyde, who embodies all of his darkest desires and fantasies.

After Sir Charles threatens to end Jeckyll's engagement to Beatrix, the Doctor seeks relief from the pressure. He has been working long hours and his most trusted peers feel he has gone too far. Tired of being proper, mannered and responsible, Jeckyll takes the chemical to transform into Mr. Hyde and goes out for a wild night on the town.

Soon, he cannot control his behavior, transforms without the drugs and goes mad, leading Mr. Hyde to kidnap a barmaid, Ivy (Ingrid Bergman), who he helped save from a previous attacker.

### *Will Jeckyll be able to control his wild side?*

### *Will he be able to marry Beatrix?*

### *Will he kill Ivy or someone else?*

Tracy was the perfect choice for the film after displaying great versatility playing both mob tough guys (*Up the River*) and a clergy man (*Boys Town*). He was one of the few actors in Hollywood who could convincingly play good and evil without driving the audience away. Tracy particularly shines as Mr. Hyde. With the help of some great make up, he is able to play a wild, Neanderthal man driven by primal urges. Tracy is so adept at playing the evil villain that you will probably have a hard time believing that it's him. He is frightening.

This was a big role for Lana Turner. After being discovered in Schwab's drugstore while sipping a soda at the counter, Turner became known as "The Sweater Girl" because she was wearing a tight fitting, sexy sweater at the time—an outfit she would wear in many of her films. After starring in such romps as *Dancing Co-Ed*, *These Glamour Girls*, *Love Finds Andy Hardy* and *Ziegfeld Girl*, Turner wanted to breakout from her image as a "sweater sweetheart". This role gave her that opportunity and helped transform her into a more glamorous star.

Ingrid Bergman also deserves kudos for her role. She plays the sexy barmaid from the wrong side of town that stirs Dr. Jeckyll's passions. Early in the movie, she is in control and using her feminine wiles to seduce the Doctor, but later in the film, she cowers and pleads for the mercy of a mad man. It is a daring character considering that the studio, after this film, started to promote her as a wholesome role model throughout the 40's even as she appeared in such a scandalous role in *Notorious*.

Bergman achieved great success on the Swedish screen throughout the 30's, which led legendary producer David O. Selznick to bring her to America. She appeared in several films before starring in Casablanca. In the late forties, she was taken with the work of Italian director Roberto Rosellini. She wrote him a letter asking to work with him.

In 1949, Bergman shocked the world by leaving her husband and young daughter for Rossellini as they were making the film *Stromboli*. She was pregnant with Rossellini's son. The events almost destroyed her career as religious groups, women's clubs and politicians criticized her publicly. One Senator claimed on the senate floor that Bergman was, "Hollywood's apostle of degradation" and "a free love cultist." The charges came during the 1950's red scare, a time when all public figures were under extreme scrutiny for any communist or anti-American sentiment, especially foreigners. Bergman's career was destroyed until her Oscar winning comeback in 1956's *Anastasia*. Her marriage to Rossellini was annulled in 1958, but yielded that son and two daughters, one of whom is Isabella Rossellini. She later married a Swedish stage producer, but they divorced in 1975.

If you want to view a traditional Hollywood horror film this weekend, rent *Dr. Jeckyll and Mr. Hyde*.

# *The Hand*

◆

## *Starring Michael Caine*

What better way to celebrate Halloween than to rent a scary horror film? There are many gory films to choose from, but I prefer a film that gets inside your head rather than splashing blood and guts all across the screen. Alfred Hitchcock was a master at this type of film. He could make you jump out of your skin by showing the audience what was going to happen, then implying the violence or scary part. Hitchcock made you more frightened watching the protagonist walking up the stairs to sure doom than watching someone get hacked up.

*The Hand* is a Hitchcock-type horror film written and directed by Oliver Stone before he became a star. Many people remember when Oliver Stone burst on the scene with 1984's *Platoon*, but he was an accomplished screenwriter before that. He wrote *Scarface*, *Midnight Express* and *Conan the Barbarian*. During this period of his career, he wrote and directed *The Hand*. He even appears on screen during the film. See if you can pick him out.

Michael Caine stars as Jonathan Lansdale, a successful cartoonist and failed husband. His wife, Anne (Andrea Marcovicci), wants to move to New York and pursue her own career. The marriage is strained by her desire to grow and his controlling tendencies, but Jonathan's career is destroyed, when his hand is severed in a car accident. His wife tries to find the hand, so it can be reattached, but she is unsuccessful.

Jonathan's agent wants the comic strip to continue with a new artist (Charles Fleisher AKA Roger Rabbit), and Anne wants the money, but

Jonathan is not willing to give up control. His marriage is further damaged by his desire to move to California and accept a teaching job.

The stress starts to effect Jonathan and results in him experiencing "blackouts". Strange things start to happen, like his ring disappears and art boards are destroyed. Soon, people who have upset Jonathan start to disappear.

***Is he committing these acts, or has his severed hand reanimated to cause havoc?***

Michael Caine is fantastic in the film. He plays the character as an arrogant jerk who seems to be losing control of his temper as his life erodes around him. Caine is able to show how deeply disturbed the man is and he allows his anger to consume him.

Stone put together a great script. The audience is left to wonder throughout the movie if The Hand is alive or a figment of Lansdale's imagination. You will be guessing right up until the final scene.

# Never Cry Wolf

## Starring Charles Martin Smith

He is one of those actors who you always recognize, but never know his name. He was in *Deep Impact, Speechless, The Untouchables, Starman* and *The Buddy Holly Story*, but Charles Martin Smith will always be remembered as Ron Howard's buddy in *American Graffiti*. Smith has had a long and distinguished career in Hollywood. Part of his career that is not known to many people is the amazing movie, *Never Cry Wolf*.

In this film, the Arctic's Caribou population is rapidly dwindling, and wolves are being blamed. No one has seen a wolf kill a caribou, so authorities send Tyler (Charles Martin Smith) out into the wilderness to witness the act, so they can be justified in killing off the wolf population. Tyler is a biologist bureaucrat who fills out reports in triplicate, not a survival expert, but he accepts the assignment to satisfy his intellectual curiosity.

With a small amount of supplies, Tyler makes his way into the arctic. Unlike the world he is accustomed to, man is meaningless in this area. Other animals barely pay attention to him. In many ways, he is just another animal in the ecosystem. Worse yet, he is the freshest piece of meat for the next predator who finds him.

Every evening, he hears the wolves, but never sees them. Soon, he is having nightmares about being attacked by them. One evening, a mysterious dogsledder finds his camp and moves him to a better one near the wolves, hoping it will help his study. Tyler soon finds the target of his investigation, a white wolf he names George.

Tyler and George engage in a battle of wits and wills as he tries to study the wolf and his habits. He grows to respect George and hopes that it is not the wolves killing off the caribou.

### *What is the truth?*

When I was in junior high school, our class watched *Never Cry Wolf*, after reading the original novel by Farley Mowat. Years later, I find myself having a different reaction to it. Maybe it is experience gained from additional years of life or a new appreciation for nature, but the movie is a moving investigation of man's frailty and vulnerability. *Never Cry Wolf* reminds us that we merely share the world with millions of other living creatures. However, we are also part of the ecosystem and must survive just like other animals.

As an actor, Smith faces a daunting task. In many scenes, he is the only human being, so he must express himself without flowing lines of dialogue. I enjoyed his performance, especially his "interaction" with George. Watch his moment of realization once Tyler has discovered what is causing the extermination of the caribou and wolves. It is an amazing plot twist.

Screenwriters Curtis Hanson and Sam Hamm deserve praise for that unexpected plot twist. I was also impressed because the movie clearly encourages viewers to have more respect for nature, but doesn't take a sanctimonious tone. The message comes through clearly without long speeches and denigration of other characters.

Another wonderful aspect to the movie is its cinematography. The entire movie was filmed in British Columbia, which provides breathtaking views of land never touched by man. I imagine the movie was even more stunning on the big screen. Some movies suffer when they move from the big screen to the little screen due to a high reliance on special effects, but this movie doesn't have that problem. It is still startling on my 19-inch television.

# *The Great Santini*

❖

## *Starring Robert Duvall, Blythe Danner and Michael O'Keefe*

*The Great Santini,* based on Pat Conroy's autobiographical novel, was *WaffleMovies.com's* first classic movie review. Most of you probably were not aware, but one of this movie's most famous scenes was satirized in *Austin Powers II: The Spy Who Shagged Me.* Rent it to see which one.

In *The Great Santini,* Robert Duvall stars as Bull Meechum, a hot shot Marine fighter pilot known for his amazing flying ability and drinking problems. He has become known by the nickname "The Great Santini" because he is considered the best pilot in the Corps, but his behavior and drinking has marred a great career and caused him to be passed over for promotion. It's 1962 and, since the country is not at war, Bull has too much time on his hands. He is a tough Marine who misbehaves and causes mischief like a teenager. In Spain, he has been causing havoc and upsetting his superiors. Even Bull realizes he is, "a warrior without a war."

Bull is transferred stateside to Beufort, SC to train an underachieving squadron of pilots. He is excited to return to the states and reunite with his family. On the surface, his family seems to be glad to have him back, but we soon learn that Bull has a strained relationship with them. He treats the children like his troops; ordering them around, having inspections and chastising them like a drill sergeant. The children resent the Marine life and wish they could have a more loving father.

Bull also is slowly being replaced as the man in of the house. His oldest son, Ben (Michael O'Keefe), is approaching his eighteenth birthday. He is becoming a man with his own set of values, which causes him to clash with his overbearing father. Now that Ben is an adult, he realizes that things should be different and his father needs to shape up. Bull continues to push Ben to join the Marines, but he wants to go his own way.

### *Who will win the battle of wills?*

Duvall and O'Keefe both give stunning performances. Duvall gives the character life by showing Bull's almost psychotic behavior, but balances it with tender scenes. At one point in the movie, Bull realizes everything that he has done wrong. Duvall is brilliant in this heart-wrenching epiphany.

O'Keefe, who you will recognize from *Caddyshack*, does a great job as Ben, especially opposite the fantastic performance by Duvall. While Duvall is the star of the movie, *The Great Santini* is about Ben's coming of age. O'Keefe shows the vulnerability of his character and the love he has for his father. He balances his rebellion with caring, respect and fear. It's a difficult part, but O'Keefe is up to the task.

Two other performances also stand out. The first is by Blythe Danner. Many of you probably know her as Gwyneth Paltrow's mom, but she is an accomplished actress. In *The Great Santini*, she plays Bull's apologetic wife, Lillian. Danner's character, like O'Keefe's, walks a fine line between love and hate for Bull. She deftly portrays the character's strength, but also her denial about Bull's behavior.

Another actress who deserves praise is Lisa Jane Persky, who plays the oldest daughter, Mary Anne. She is the family member with the most anger and animosity towards her father. She wants a loving, caring father and mocks Bull for his lack of those traits. In many ways, she is the only character who does not apologize for Bull.

Since *The Great Santini*, Duvall has continued his stellar career, Danner has raised an Academy Award winner, O'Keefe has starred in several smaller movies, and Pat Conroy has gone on to write the best selling novels *The Prince Of Tides* and *Beach Music*. Although the film came out almost twenty years ago, audiences of today can relate and enjoy this classic.

# *Christmas Eve*

◆

## *Starring Loretta Young*

There are very few legends left from Hollywood's golden age. Humphrey Bogart, Clark Gable, Spencer Tracy, Carole Lombard, Ingrid Bergman and more passed away years ago. Recently, one woman who rose to stardom during Hollywood's golden age, then television's golden age, left us. Christmas Eve, an NBC movie of the week in 1986, was one of Loretta Young's final performances.

Young stars as Amanda Kingsley, the widow of a powerful and very rich businessman. While her son, Andrew (Arthur Hill), runs the multi-million dollar company founded by the family, she continues to hold 51% percent of the stock. Amanda has final approval of all business matters.

Unfortunately, Amanda and Andrew do not see eye to eye. She is a very giving and caring person who wanders the streets of New York late at night with her butler, Maitland (Trevor Howard), giving cash to the homeless and taking in stray cats. This drives her son crazy. Amanda decides that she must teach her cold, unloving son how to care for others, so she hires a detective, Morris Huffner (Ron Liebman), to track down his estranged children in time for them to come home for Christmas. However, the holiday might be spoiled when Andrew decides to take his mother to court and get her declared mentally incompetent because she has changed her will to exclude him from taking control of the company when she dies. Instead, Amanda wants to set up a foundation to build shelters for homeless people.

*Will Amanda's grandchildren return home for Christmas?*

*Will she be declared incompetent?*

The movie is a good Christmas weeper. Young is lovable as the kindly grandmother and philanthropist who wants to help the less fortunate, including her own family. Trevor Howard is funny as the bumbling butler and confidant, while Arthur Hill is passable as the stereotypical Scrooge who needs to learn his lesson. The plot doesn't have too many surprises, but what do you want? It's a Christmas movie!

Young was always known as one of America's most proper actresses. She was devoutly catholic and often imposed fines on those who used profane language on the set of her television program. However, one mystery always haunted her, and, was finally put to rest after her death.

After filming the 1935 movie *Call of the Wild* with actor Clark Gable, Young withdrew from public life. When she re-emerged, she adopted a baby girl, Judy. However, Judy didn't need to be adopted.

Before her death in August, 2000, Young confirmed a long believed rumor to her biographer—she disappeared from public life to give birth to Judy, even though she was not married. On a train ride in 1935, Young shared a night of passion with her *Call of the Wild* co-star, Clark Gable. Young got pregnant, but feared the negative publicity, so she devised the plan where she would adopt Judy to cover up the pregnancy and her relationship with Clark Gable.

Even Judy had suspicions about her real mother and father, especially when the rumor would never go away. We don't know if Gable ever knew about his daughter. One can only hope that he did. After the tragic death of his wife, Carole Lombard, Gable was shattered. He turned to alcohol, his career suffered and he died in 1960 before his only other child, a son, was born.

Young was correct to fear the negative fallout that would have resulted if she revealed the extra-marital relations. Because her entire image had been rooted in her wholesomeness, and America was not accepting of having babies out of wedlock (especially from those who were as religious as Young), she would have been ruined, much like Ingrid Bergman had been in 1949 when she had an affair with Roberto Rosselini. Instead, she was able to go on to star in many movies and a very successful television program.

If you want a little sappy sentimentality this weekend, try Christmas Eve.

# Holiday Affair

### Starring Robert Mitchum and Janet Leigh

In 1949's Holiday Affair, Janet Leigh (yes, Jamie Lee Curtis' mom) (yes, Janet Leigh from Psycho) stars as a war widow, Connie, who is trying to make ends meet by working as a department store comparison shopper. She goes from store to store to gather prices and samples of other products, so her employer can do it better and cheaper. Unfortunately, she is too honest and clumsy to be very good at it.

One day, she wanders into a competitor's toy department to investigate their hot new toy trains and gets discovered by Steve Mason (Robert Mitchum). He takes pity on her and refuses to turn her in. Along the way, Steve gets to know her better and falls in love with Connie. There is just one, big problem.

Connie is engaged to be married to Carl (Wendell Corey) on New Year's Day. He is a decent fellow who is despised by her 6-year old son. Although the situation leaves a little something to be desired, Connie marches on with hopes that her son will start to like Carl.

### Will Steve steal Connie away from Carl?

### What will Steve's boss think when he discovers that Steve has been helping the enemy?

Robert Mitchum didn't do many romantic comedies, but his natural, roguish charm comes in handy. Although the audience should despise him for trying to steal another's man's fiancée, Steve is much more likable than Carl because Mitchum uses his smoky eyes and wry smile to win us over. It is a smooth, almost effortless, performance that was a wonderful contrast to the many war films with which he established his career.

Janet Leigh is wonderful filling a new role for women of the late 40's. She represented the many war widows who suddenly found themselves struggling to make a living and provide a traditional upbringing for their children. It was a difficult time that doesn't get much attention in films or in the history books.

If you're looking for a fun, breezy romantic comedy that will warm the heart during the holiday season, rent *Holiday Affair* with someone you love. It gets a little slow in the middle, but pays off in the end.

*The Independents*

# *Just Write*

### *Starring Jeremy Piven and Sherilyn Fenn*

Every book has to start somewhere, so I decided to start with a film that exemplifies the spirit of *WaffleMovies.com and Backshelf Beauties*.

For every surprise smash film like *Blair Witch Project,* there are hundreds of others that never break through. That was why I started *WaffleMovies.com* and why I wrote this book. I wanted to bring attention to wonderful movies that didn't get the credit and attention they deserved. *Just Write* is a perfect example of the type of movie I want you to enjoy, so, take a chance this week by running down to the video store and renting it (However, there is no money back guarantee, so don't start calling me looking for your refund. I've got a book but not the bucks.). Just because the movie didn't star Tom Cruise and didn't make $100 Million at the box office shouldn't disqualify it as a great work. I am proud to make it the first movie I recommend to you in this book.

Jeremy Piven stars as Harold, the driver at his family's financially troubled Hollywood trolley tour business. Harold is a romantic at heart and lover of movies who wishes to meet a woman who is looking for more than a man with the perfect car and a big fat bank account. In Hollywood, this is a monumental task.

Harold decides to visit his friend Danny (Jeffrey Sams), a bartender at a trendy Hollywood watering hole. At the bar, he meets Amanda Clark (Sherilyn Fenn), the up-and-coming star that everyone is talking about. Amanda is about to be named the co-star in a film with Brad Pitt, but has reservations. She doesn't like the script or the portrayal of her character, but when did this every stop an actor from taking a film that could lead to big money?

After Harold misrepresents himself as a famous screenwriter with a powerful agent, she asks him to read the script and give his "professional" opinion. When Amanda hears that he shares the same reservations, she asks him to rewrite the script.

### Can Harold fix the script and get the girl of his dreams?

Many of you may be groaning because you feel this is a formulaic romantic comedy with predictable plot twists. If that's how you feel, then I feel sorry that you will miss out on a very funny and engaging movie. It is formulaic, but the formula works as well as the secret recipe for Coca-Cola or McDonald's secret sauce. *Just Write* is a fun movie that stands out in a sea of drivel. Let those other movies have all the sex and violence, this one has heart.

After speaking with executive producer Jim Kreutzer, I love this movie even more. *Just Write* is the little movie that could. It was financed by seven Wisconsin dentists who wanted to make a quality movie they could be proud of. They put an advertisement in the *Hollywood Reporter* soliciting scripts and, after receiving over 500 works, chose Stan Williamson's romantic comedy due to its positive nature and uplifting message.

After choosing a script, the production was set into motion. According to Kreutzer, many Hollywood stars wanted to participate in the project. With only $1.2 Million spend, the stars of the film had to take drastic pay cuts. Thanks to their dedication and sacrifice, the movie was made in just 19 days, and within the tight budget.

Unfortunately, there wasn't more money available to advertise the film and distribute it widely. A major studio expressed interest in releasing it straight to video, but the producers stuck to their guns. The movie opened in several markets, including Milwaukee and Dallas-Ft. Worth, where the per-screen average rivaled any major studio film. *Just Write* was the winner of several film festivals, including the Santa Bar-

bara Film Festival. It had success overseas, became a feature movie on airline flights across America, and premiered on cable in November of 1999.

Rent *Just Write* and enjoy an old fashioned Hollywood fairy tale.

# *Rosewood*

◆

## *Starring Ving Rhames, Don Cheadle, Esther Rolle and Jon Voight*

In 1923, the town of Rosewood, Florida was the site of a massacre. This sad chapter in American history wasn't learned until 60 years later when a reporter for the *St. Petersburg Times* and the son of a survivor joined forces to tell the horrible truth.

*Rosewood* tells the horrific tale of how 40-150 African-Americans were lynched, beaten and murdered when a white woman falsely accused a African-American man of attacking her. It is one of the most powerful and disturbing movies of the 90's.

The film opens in the small town of Rosewood, Florida. Most of the businesses and property are owned by African-Americans, except the town store, owned and run by Mr. Wright (Jon Voight). He has earned the respect and trust of the town's residents for doing business with them when most white merchants refuse. Mr. Wright plans on staying in Rosewood, purchasing more land, and expanding his business. Although he is well liked, he's not perfect. Mr. Wright is carrying on an affair with one of his African-American employees and still has moments when he expresses his own racism.

On New Year's Eve, a mysterious stranger comes to town. Mr. Mann (Ving Rhames) creates quite a stir in this small town. He attracts the attention of everyone, especially a young lady, Scrappy (Elise Neal). While he decides if he wants to stay permanently, Mr. Mann finds temporary residence with Scrappy, Sara (Esther Rolle), Sylvester (Don Cheadle) and their family.

Racial tensions run high between Rosewood and the neighboring white town of Sumner. These problems explode when a white woman, Fannie (Catherine Kellner) falsely claims to have been attacked by an African-American stranger, possibly an escaped convict being sought by the local sheriff (Michael Rooker). A white mob forms to find the phantom attacker, and Mr. Mann is accused by white and African-American residents of the county.

### *Did Mr. Mann do it? What will happen to Rosewood?*

After seeing the fine performances and excellent direction, I was left to wonder why the movie was overlooked by the Motion Picture Academy. There are several Oscar worthy performances. The list of actors and actresses who deliver fantastic performances is too long to mention, but five jump out immediately.

Ving Rhames is excellent as Mr. Mann, the mysterious stranger with a dark past. Rhames is able to win the audience's sympathy and respect by showing his character's cynical side and desire to live without trouble. Although his character is an honored war veteran, white men treat him horribly. Watch his reactions when he is considered a suspect by other African American residents. Mr. Mann knows he cannot trust white men, but in that moment, his character feels that he can't even trust his own people.

Don Cheadle and Esther Rolle also shine as mother and son facing possible death and ruination of their way of life. Even though her character knows the truth, Rolle is able to show how the character is afraid to step forward and tell the truth, a feeling shared by actual survivors of the Rosewood massacre. Her best scene comes when she confronts the mob and tries to set them straight before they do more damage.

Cheadle is one of my favorite actors. He consistently delivers stunning performances. His character is a proud music teacher who wants the respect he has earned. Cheadle is able to express his character's frustration and the pain he feels as his community is destroyed by ignorance and hate.

Jon Voight and Michael Rooker also put in fine performances. Voight is able to show his character's sensitivity, but also the racism that runs through him even though he is supposed to be friendly to the community. Rooker is fantastic as the town sheriff who doesn't believe that an African-American man committed the illegal act, but goes along with the mob in a fruitless attempt to avoid bloodshed.

I also want to put in a word for director John Singleton. Many of you probably remember that he was the first African American nominated as Best Director for his groundbreaking film, *Boyz 'n the Hood*. In this film, he shows great ability to tell a painful story on a grand scale. Although the film is almost 2 ½ hours long, he keeps the pace moving and riveting. He uses wonderful, sweeping shots of the landscape to show the town's destruction and gets amazing performances out of every actor.

The story of Rosewood was a secret until 1982, when Gray Moore of the *St. Petersburg Times* visited the Rosewood area. He wondered why there were few African-American resident of Levy County, so he started an investigation. Moore found survivors of the massacre who had lost their personal wealth and families, but they did not want to talk for fear of retribution.

Finally, 20 survivors and their descendents were convinced to speak with Moore. They shocked him with their story. Arnette Doctor, the son of a survivor, was also researching the town's past and seeking reparations from the state legislature. They teamed up to tell the story, eventually getting the attention of CBS' *60 Minutes*. In 1994, the Florida State Legislature offered reparations to survivors and their families.

Rent *Rosewood* tonight.

# The Gun in Betty Lou's Handbag

## Starring Penelope Ann Miller and Alfre Woodard

Penelope Ann Miller is one of those actresses who could have been famous. You know what I'm talking about. You've seen her in enough movies to recognize her, but she always ends up in some flop (like *The Shadow*) instead of a blockbuster. You probably don't even remember this hidden gem from 1992, but I highly recommend taking a chance on this hilarious comedy.

Miller plays meek and mild librarian Betty Lou Perkins. She is a wallflower who is pushed around by her boss (Marian Seldes), her cop husband (Eric Thal) and even the supermarket cashier. She desperately wants to break out and become an aggressive, tough woman, but never finds the courage to do it. Betty Lou finally reaches her breaking point when husband Alex skips out on their special anniversary dinner to investigate the murder of underworld pawn Amos (Stanley Tucci).

Betty Lou accidentally sees Alex's car at the hotel where Amos was murdered, and fears Alex may be having an affair. After overhearing intimate details of the murder, she soon learns that he is just investigating the case and holds enough info to cause trouble later.

Then, Betty Lou serendipitously finds the murder weapon and, in a fit of rage, shoots out the ladies bathroom mirror in the library. The police arrest her and quickly discover that she is in possession of the murder weapon, which makes her a prime suspect, but her husband does not believe she is capable of committing the crime. Betty Lou realizes that people's opinions about her change when they think she has committed the murder, so she pleads guilty.

She quickly becomes the talk of the town as she sheds her milk toast image and people start believing that Betty Lou is dangerous, cunning and tough. Soon, she finds herself in over her head as her husband becomes estranged, and she is chased by mobsters who believe she holds incriminating evidence against their boss (William Forsyth).

### *Will Betty Lou fess up?*

Miller is hilarious as the newly empowered Betty Lou. After showing such great promise in *Biloxi Blues* and *Awakenings*, it is a shame that Miller's career has faltered. She shows great comedic ability and steals the show as Betty Lou's new personality emerges. Miller is supported by terrific performances by Julianne Moore as her best friend, Eleanor, and Alfre Woodard as her lawyer, Anne Orkin.

The movie is best when it is a farce, but director Allen Moyle and writer Grace Cary Bickley inject heavy drama by miscasting and misusing William Forsythe as mobster Billy Beaudeen. His plot and character are too heavy for this comedy and take the movie in an interesting, but somewhat unsatisfying direction. The film would have been a little better if Billy was just as kooky as the rest of the cast.

Before you think Moyle did a bad job directing, think again. Moyle makes some good decisions, such as a section of the film where the townspeople each give interviews about Betty Lou. The screenplay does a great job of tying together all the loose ends, and the movie runs at a quick, interesting pace. Instead of trying to milk out another 10—15 minutes of film, Moyle tells a tight, precise story.

After such a promising movie, many of the players' careers have stalled. Moyle went on to direct 1995's *Empire Records* starring Liv Tyler. Miller shined in 1992's *Chaplin*, but also found herself in duds *The Relic*, *The Shadow* and *Little City*. Bickley dropped out of sight until contributing to the 2002 movie, *High Crimes* (which may send her back into hiding). That's a shame, because the team delivered a fine comedy. It was also fun to watch an early performance by Moore, who has gone on to a stellar career.

Word of warning, you should know that the movie has some violent scenes, so rent with caution.

# Grace of My Heart

## Starring Illeana Douglas, Matt Dillon, John Turturro and Patsy Kensit

A desire to follow our dreams burns in each of us as we yearn to do what makes us happy and loved. Lots of us have struggled for years to build up a business or second career, and others are still struggling along. *Grace of My Heart* is the touching story of a young woman in the 1950's who disregards the insurmountable odds to seek fame and fortune in the music business.

Illeana Douglas stars as Edna Buxton, the daughter of a rich, successful family. Edna's domineering mother (Christina Pickles) doesn't want her to pursue her dream of a musical career, but Edna insists. She enters a local singing competition that awards the winner a recording contract, wins the competition, and moves to New York in, what she feels, is the first step to success.

However, things don't quite work out in New York. Edna soon learns the recording contract is a sham, but is too proud to admit failure. She embarks on a singing career, but faces great resistance from managers and agents who think male vocal bands are all the rage. Edna is on the verge of giving up when she meets Joel Millner (John Turturro). While Joel doesn't want to sign her as a singer, he recognizes Edna's writing talent. He soon convinces her to move into the legendary Brill Building, change her name to Denise Waverly, and start writing tunes for others. Denise/Edna becomes a success, but soon gets torn into other directions by the men in her life.

***As her career goes into decline, can Denise/Edna find another hit song to propel her back to the top?***

Loosely based on the life of Carole King, *Grace of My Heart* is a music history lesson. The audience is taken on a ride that spans the carefree early days of rock and roll, the corporatization of the business and the singer/songwriter revolution. Many of the other characters in the movie also are loosely based on key music industry figures, which makes the film fun for those who are familiar with music. If you think 'N Sync, The Backstreet Boys and Brittany Spears are annoying little brats, you probably like this music and this movie. Even if you don't know the history, you'll still enjoy the motley crew of hucksters, prima donnas and leeches that make up the film's view of the music industry.

The movie is also a study in the difficulties of women in the workplace. Denise/Edna faces great opposition as she attempts to find success in a male dominated business. She also is lead to failure by the men in her life who do not allow her to rely on her own instincts and talents. While the movie inspires everyone to follow their own heart, it particularly instructs women to rely on their instincts to find success.

Illeana Douglas must have followed her own instincts because the role is very different from her previous work. She plays a character that is much more vulnerable than others she has portrayed, and I think it works well. She puts in a good performance and particularly shines towards the end of the movie, when it appears her career is over. Douglas perfectly captures the despair her character is feeling as she faces the end.

While the movie is a star vehicle for Douglas, it is John Turturro as the fast talking, hyperactive manger who steals the show. Of all the men in Edna/Denise's life, Millner is the one who truly cares for her and never abandons her or her dream of becoming a singer. Turturro portrays the character with a zeal, cockiness and bravado that you would expect from a successful rock and roll producer. He plays the character well for comic relief when needed, but also as a strong, loving friend.

The movie marks a return by writer/director Allison Anders to the investigation of women's lives in America. She should be applauded for that effort. Movies should be about more than making money (a statement that will get you kicked out of the corporate boardrooms of the big conglomerates that run the studios these days). Movies can be an escape for the audience, but they also can make a statement about the society we live in. Clearly, there is room for both.

*Grace of My Heart* is fantastic for the first three-quarters, takes a strange detour, but returns to leave the audience satisfied in the end. The film has a great soundtrack featuring music by Elvis Costello and Burt Bacharach. Before rewinding it, check out the video for "God Give Me Strength" at the end of the tape. It is much better than the version performed in the movie. Also, keep your eyes open for surprise cameos by current music and movie stars.

# *This is My Father*

*Starring James Caan, Aidan Quinn, Moya Farrelly and Colm Meaney*

We all have a need to know about our family history. I have always believed that one cannot know where the future leads without knowing about the past. Our family history defines us and instructs us in our everyday lives. We can learn many lessons from those who passed through this world before (especially pay attention to anything Michael Jackson has done and do the opposite). This Saint Patrick's Day, settle down with this beautiful Irish tale.

James Caan stars as Kieren, a bitter widowed teacher. He has never met his father and doesn't know anything about the man who gave him life. His mother has suffered a stroke and doesn't interact with the family anymore, so Kieren fears that he will never learn about his father now that his mother cannot communicate.

One afternoon, he stumbles across some old photos and letters in his mother's attic. They are from the 1930's and look like they might be the key to the mystery. Kieren decides to travel to Ireland and find the truth about his father. Maybe he is still alive?

### *Will Kieren find his father?*

James Caan gets to show a tender side in this movie that you don't normally see. His character longs for the truth about his lineage and hopes to teach his nephew (Jacob Tierney) a valuable lesson. Caan is wonderful as he struggles with his classroom of misfits, a nephew who is getting into trouble and a disabled mother. I hope Caan takes more of these roles.

Moya Farrelly and Aidan Quinn make the movie interesting in a flashback technique that might hold the key to the mystery. The tale of their long ago love affair is riveting. We have often seen this type of plot before; older man having a relationship with a younger woman who is mature and wise beyond her years. However, Quinn and Farrelly have great chemistry and both play their parts perfectly. Quinn makes Kieren into a slow minded, but pure of heart decent man wanting no more out of life than a wife and farm. Farrelly makes her character into a brash, rebellious, adventurous young lady hoping to start a new life in America. The two open up new worlds to each other.

The making of *This is My Father* is a family affair. It marks the writing and directing debut of Aidan Quinn's brother, Paul Quinn. He spent six months in Ireland and that experience, teamed with a similar story his mother used to tell him, inspired Quinn to write the movie. However, he put it aside for ten years after he returned to America. After completing the script, he gave it to brothers Aidan and director of photography Declan Quinn to read and critique. Paul feared they might not like it, but they enthusiastically backed the project.

At a time when most movies are geared to the teeny-bopper set, it is refreshing to see a mature movie. You'll love this touching tale and its gorgeous scenery. The entire movie was filmed in Ireland and you get to see some of the most beautiful lush scenery on the planet.

# The Imposters

❖

## Starring Stanley Tucci, Oliver Platt, Hope Davis, Steve Buscemi and Tony Shalhoub

A ship of fools bound for Paris serves as the madcap setting in this hilarious homage to the great Depression-era Marx Brothers movies. This little gem also serves as the perfect antidote to a summer full of loud, massive, over-hyped productions.

In a movie written and directed by Stanley Tucci, Oliver Platt and Tucci star as two down on their luck Depression-era actors struggling to survive without leaving the profession. Maurice (Platt) and Arthur (Tucci) can only secure one audition, which falls through before they can even finish their scene. In a fit of desperation, they formulate a scheme to get some food, but it backfires when it only yields two tickets to *Hamlet* starring an actor they despise, Jeffrey Burtom (Alfred Molina).

After the play, they meet with one of their fellow actors who is in the production, and jealously rage about Burtom's performance and fame. Unfortunately, Burtom enters the same bar and gets into a scuffle with our heroes. The police instantly assume Maurice and Arthur are at fault, which leads to a manhunt. To escape, they hide in a crate, which ends up being loaded onto a cruise ship bound for Paris and carrying none other than Jeffrey Burtom.

**Can these two sad sacks pull off the performance of their lives to avoid arrest, stop the murder of two passengers and save the ship from a mad bomber?**

The movie is crowded with imposters; two scam artists trying to rob and kill two passengers, suicidal crooner "Happy" Franks, a deposed queen who has fled her country, a mad bomber posing as the ship's first mate, and a widow who has lost all of her wealth

There are some wonderful performances in the movie that deserve praise. Stanley Tucci is fantastic as Arthur. He has great comedic timing, good chemistry with co-star Platt and will tickle your funny bone with his hilarious facial expressions. Platt and Tucci also take advantage of their "Mutt and Jeff" type status to engage in some good old-fashioned physical comedy.

What makes the movie enjoyable is the performance of the supporting cast. Steve Buscemi as Happy Franks is not given enough of a chance to show his abilities here, but takes what little he has and steals every scene he is in. Hope Davis shows she is more than just a pretty face (but, I want to mention this if she is reading the book, still a very beautiful face) as her character, Emily, falls for the suicidal crooner and tries to make him see life is worth living.

Other supporting players shine as well. Billy Connolly takes a hilarious turn as Mr. Sparks, the man who makes Maurice the object of his affection. Campbell Scott tears it up as German crewmember Meistrich, who is hopelessly in love with Maurice and Arthur's protector, Lilly (Lili Taylor). Alfred Molina shines as the pompous, drunken Jeffrey Burtom, and Matt McGrath holds his own in this star studded cast as Marco, the crew member with a heart of gold who cannot follow through on his orders to kill our two heroes.

If you want to take a break from the futuristic summer blockbusters, take a chance on this throwback to great madcap physical comedy. Even with a few flaws, it is better than most movies you will find in the theater or on video.

# *Waiting for Guffman*

### *Starring Christopher Guest, Eugene Levy, Parker Posey and Catherine O'Hara*

Sometimes, you need a silly, funny movie to cheer you up. Lucky for us, Christopher Guest (*Saturday Night Live, This is Spinal Tap*) has created just such a laugh riot in *Waiting for Guffman*.

Co-writer and director Guest portrays off-off-off-Broadway dancer Corky St. John. Corky has moved to Blaine, MO to escape a lackluster, failed career in New York. However, Broadway still burns in his blood, so he forms the Blaine Community players theater group. To celebrate the town's one hundred-fiftieth anniversary, he writes the musical Red, White and Blaine, a tale of the town's history. The town's hopes and dreams soon come to life as they receive word that Broadway producer Mort Guffman will be coming to Blaine to review the play.

### *Can Corky and the gang impress Guffman enough to win a chance at fame and fortune?*

Guest creates a farcical town and people. By using a documentary style, he allows the actors to create quirky characters who reveal their thoughts by speaking directly to us. We learn that Blaine was settled in 1845, when Blaine Faban was hired to lead an expedition from Philadelphia to California, but was unable to get the group across country. The town finds fame in 1898 when President McKinley is presented with a footstool manufactured in Blaine. The town soon becomes a stool-manufacturing powerhouse. Then, in 1946, Blaine claims to achieve first contact with aliens when they land in town and invite the citizens of Blaine to a potluck supper.

This strange lineage explains why the town is full of imbeciles. Each character is taken to new heights of foolishness by this talented, veteran cast. Each character is well defined by strong performances and excellent writing. Co-writer Eugene Levy plays Dr. Allen Pearl, the local dentist who secretly yearns to be a star. Levy is fantastic as he plays one of the movie's silliest characters in an understated, reserved manner. Joining Levy is the always wonderful Parker Posey, who portrays Dairy Queen employee Libby Mae Brown, a girl who just wants to go to New York to meet boys. Fred Willard and Catherine O'Hara play the town's travel agents and Hepburn and Tracy wannabes, Ron and Sheila Albertson. Other performers who deserve special recognition are Michael Hitchcock who plays the role of Councilman Stark, a local pharmacist who seems to be very attracted to Corky, and Bob Balaban who plays jealous music teacher Lloyd Miller.

After starring in and co-writing the uproarious *This is Spinal Tap*, Christopher Guest is no stranger to mockumentaries. He reunites with former partners Harry Shearer and Michael McKean to create the hysterical tunes performed in Red, White and Blaine. Many will recognize the movie's allusion to the play *Waiting for Godo*. Like *Godo*, the citizens of Blaine anxiously await the appearance of Mort Guffman, which provides the movie's funniest plot twists.

*Waiting for Guffman* was nominated for Best Actor (Guest), Best Movie and Best Screenplay at the Independent Spirit Awards in 1998. After watching the movie, I am sure you will whole-heartedly agree with the selection committee.

For a fun-filled, hilarious evening, rent *Waiting for Guffman*.

# *Swingers*

### *Starring Jon Favreau, Vince Vaughn and Heather Graham*

The 90's brought many movies dealing with the relationships between men and women. Instead of being romantic comedies, they are psychological examinations filled with Tarantino-esque hip dialogue. I guess that's because every generation thinks their battle of the sexes is somehow different from earlier ones. That, or those of us in our late 20's and early 30's are more prone to self-loathing. Some of these movies didn't hit the mark, but many are among the best movies of the decade. *Swingers* stands out as a classic.

Screenwriter Jon Favreau plays Michael, a down-on-his-luck actor/comedian who left New York for the fame and fortune of Tinseltown. According to Michael, "they made it sound as if they were handing out sit-coms to comedians at the airport." He's had some small roles, and hosts open mic night at a local comedy club, but Michael doesn't feel successful, because he had to break up with his girlfriend of six years when he came to Los Angeles, and never moved on. He still loves her, and let's everyone know it.

His friends want to help him move on, especially Trent (Vince Vaughn) who takes him on a wild, hilarious trip to Las Vegas. Trent's a player with his hyperactive speech pattern and charismatic ways. Women flock to him and, when he's around, fun is not far away. After a series of disasters and near misses, Michael finally finds the courage to get a woman's phone number.

## *Will he blow it?*

*Swingers* is one of the funniest, best written movies around. My friends and I find ourselves constantly quoting dialogue from the movie and watching it several times a year. Favreau brilliantly satirizes the dating scene, and exposes it for all it shallowness and mocks its "rules".

The movie also is a great send up of Hollywood. The characters struggle to get bit parts and commiserate with each other by sharing their tales of woe. Each one wants to be a big star, but they have to take other odd jobs to get by. By far, the best tale is Rob's (Ron Livingston) struggles with Disneyland and the opinions each person has about which theme park character is the best to portray. After working for Disney, I found a whole new appreciation for this scene.

Each character also tries to be Mr. Cool. One of the most entertaining parts of the movie is watching each of these vulnerable, clumsy guys try to be slick and smooth, while lacking the confidence to do so. I guess that's why women laugh at us in bars and clubs (they laugh at all of us, right? It's not just me?).

Vince Vaughn is the star of the movie. While Favreau is the lead, Vaughn has the most memorable performance. He is full of charisma and lights up the screen whenever he is in the scene. It takes great stamina to maintain such an energetic performance and he does it well. Unfortunately, Vaughn has not found a role since that can take advantage of his comedic ability. He has been trying to establish himself as a leading man, but might be well served to take a secondary role in a major movie to showcase his ability and attract better scripts.

Jon Favreau is very good as the comedian who never laughs. He is supposed to make his living as a funny man, but his character constantly mopes around and feels sorry for himself. Favreau is an engaging character, the friend we all want to see do well. As Vaughn's character points out, Favreau is "the guy in the PG-13 movie that we really hope makes it."

Another wonderful ingredient in this movie is the music. *Swingers* was made just as swing music was starting its resurgence and nicely captures the Los Angeles retro scene. Big Bad Voodoo Daddy contributes a few songs to the soundtrack, while the rest is filled out by classic music from Dean Martin and others. I don't normally buy movie soundtracks, but this one is good addition to the CD collection.

Instead of subjecting yourself to the bar scene this weekend, get your friends together and rent *Swingers*. Now available on DVD!

# A Walk on the Moon

◆

## Starring Diane Lane, Liev Schreiber and Viggo Mortenson

As we grow older, all of us wonder if we have made the right decisions about life (this seems to be a recurring theme with the movies I have chosen. Some psychiatrist must be reading this and looking for my phone number). We look back on the optimistic, wide-eyed innocence of our youth and see how far we are from where we thought we would be. *A Walk On The Moon* is one woman's self-exploration of her regrets and the trouble she causes by trying to escape from her current life.

Diane Lane plays Pearl, a mother and wife in her mid-thirties. Her husband Marty (Liev Schreiber), mother-in-law (Tovah Feldshuh), 14-year old daughter Allison (Anna Paquin) and young son have a cottage in upstate New York where they spend the summer. It's a quiet place surrounded by other families who are not prepared for the wild summer ahead. Set in 1969, they are located near White Lake, where the Woodstock festival is scheduled to happen. Allison is eager to have an adventurous summer and attend Woodstock, while her mother simply wants to enjoy herself and, possibly, spice up her marriage.

Pearl is going through a mid-life crisis and wonders if she made the right choices. She questions what her life could have been like if she did not make one big mistake. She feels like she missed out by never experiencing the wild life that young people around her are living. Pearl soon strikes up a relationship with the hunky, hippie blouse salesman, Walker Jerome (Viggo Mortenson) and explores her wild side during a torrid love affair with him.

### *What will Pearl do when she must face the guilt and consequences of her self-indulgence?*

Pamela Gray has written one of the best screenplays in a long time. It would be very easy to write a sappy script where Pearl is engaged in a horrible marriage and seeks refuge with the hunky, hippie blouse salesman. However, Gray makes the situation much more complicated, therefore, more interesting. Pearl and Marty have a rocky marriage, but he is a responsible, loving husband and father trying to raise his family under traditional expectations of what he is supposed to do. The audience has a natural sympathy for Marty, but can also relate to Pearl. Both of them have made mistakes and sacrifices, but they have stuck it out together. In many ways, Pearl is simply looking for the passion that they once had, however, Gray shows that the relationship has grown. It is not a passionless marriage, but a marriage with a different kind of passion.

Lane deserves praise for her difficult turn. Her character seeks unbridled passion, but must deal with the consequences of her actions. Lane sparkles in scenes with Mortenson as her character allows herself to be swept away, but also delivers in very intense scenes with Schreiber as she explains the relationship to him.

Schreiber gets the most dramatic role and doesn't disappoint. I've seen Schreiber triumphantly tackle comedy and drama, so I usually expect a good performance out of him. In *A Walk On The Moon*, he tempers his character's rage with feelings of betrayal and questions if he is to blame.

Check it out this weekend.

# *Big Night*

◆

## *Starring Stanley Tucci, Tony Shalhoub, Minnie Driver and Allison Janney*

*Big Night* is a moving look at the struggle of two Italian immigrants operating an authentic Italian restaurant on the Jersey shore in the 1950's, and their battle to maintain their principles in the face of losing everything. It is a wonderful movie that shows us how to celebrate life and live it to the fullest. The movie also addresses everyman's struggle to protect what matters most when it means the difference between success and failure.

Brothers Primo (Tony Shalhoub) and Secundo (Stanley Tucci) are the owners of a failing Italian restaurant. Primo is a brilliant, proud, but tempermental chef who refuses to compromise his art—cooking. Even though the restaurant is doing poorly and many of the customers want Americanized versions of Italian cooking, Primo refuses to change. His art is a grand tradition handed down from generation to generation. He feels, "If I sacrifice my work, it dies."

Secundo manages the restaurant and desperately wants to live the American dream. To do so, he wants to change the menu and attract more customers. He is envious of his friend Pascal (Ian Holm) who runs a very successful Italian restaurant across the street. Even though he despises the compromises that Pascal has made, Secundo wants to have the success and material wealth that Pascal does. Unfortunately, he has been informed by his bank that it will foreclose on the restaurant at the end of the month unless Primo and Secundo can pay off a loan.

Pascal recognizes the great talent that Primo and Secundo have. He even wants to hire them if they decide to give up the restaurant, so he offers to do them a favor. Pascal is a friend of famous jazz trumpeter Louis Prima. He offers to invite Louis to their restaurant in an effort to get them some attention and new customers. Pascal feels that people will go to the restaurant to see Louis Prima, but will fall in love with the cooking. Secundo is thrilled at this last attempt to succeed, and spends every last penny they have to make the evening a memorable one.

**Will the plan work? Will Louis Prima show up?**

At the center of the movie is the great talent of Stanley Tucci. Not only is he one of the stars, but he co-wrote and co-directed the film. We instantly recognize ourselves in his struggles to succeed and his loss of spirit when he works hard, but fails. Tucci commands the screen and creates a complex, but likable character. While Secundo is a hard working, honest man, he also has his flaws.

Most of you will remember Tony Shalhoub from the television shows *Wings* or *Monk*, or the movies *Men in Black* or *The Man Who Wasn't There*. This movie proves that his talent is very rarely fully utilized. Shalhoub is able to portray the great pride his character has as well as his shyness and tenderness. It's more complex than just being the butt of a joke.

The rest of the ensemble is just as brilliant. Ian Holm is fantastic as Secundo's friend Pascal. He is able to make the character lovable, but also shows his cold, conniving side as well. Pre-*Good Will Hunting* Minnie Driver plays Secundo's American girlfriend, Phyllis. She doesn't get much to do in the film, but she is strong enough and good enough stand out in scenes with Tucci.

Tucci and co-writer Joseph Tropiano have created a movie that has everything you want. There are two wonderful love stories. One involving Tucci and Driver; the other involving Shalhoub and Allison Janney who plays a local florist that Primo is too shy to ask out on a date. There is drama as we wonder if Prima will come to dinner, if the two brothers will succeed, and what will happen when they learn about their different plans for the future. There is also comedy.

Tucci and his directing partner Campbell Scott magnificently contrast the various scenes. In some scenes, the screen is filled with a loud celebration or fight between the brothers. However, other scenes convey just as much without even using a word of dialogue. It is truly a masterful movie.

# *Ulee's Gold*

### *Starring Peter Fonda, Patricia Richardson and Jessica Biel*

Some movies explode off the screen with special effects and a soundtrack that can make your eardrums hurt (anyone who went to the Doctor after seeing *XXX* or almost any Arnold Scwarzenegger movie will know what I am talking about). They grab you with their sheer volume. Other movies, like *Ulee's Gold,* are meant to be savored like a fine wine, rolled around the pallet on a moonlit evening.

In *Ulee's Gold*, writer/director Victor Nunez creates a beautiful, tender movie about Ulee the beekeeper (Peter Fonda), a strong, quiet, but passionate man who struggles to keep his family safe. We learn early in the movie that Ulee's business is struggling. He is faced with dropping prices for honey, new competition from foreign manufacturers and disease among his bees. He has reached the most important part of the season, and thinks this is his chance to get on the right track.

However, trouble strikes when he least needs it. Ulee has been raising his two granddaughters since his son was arrested in a bank robbery and his daughter-in-law ran off to Orlando. Ulee has refused to speak or have any contact with his son since he went to jail two years ago. Jimmy's daughter, Casey (Jessica Biel), has written letters to him, but they were never answered. The youngest daughter, Penny (Vanessa Zima), does not have any solid recollection of her parents.

Sadly, Jimmy's wife, Helen (Christine Dunford), has found trouble in Orlando. Jimmy calls Ulee after she wanders into a local bar, strung out on drugs. Jimmy's bank robbery accomplices, Eddie (Steven

Flynn) and Ferris (Dewey Weber) found her and have learned that Jimmy secretly took $100,000 from the bank robbery. Now, Eddie and Ferris want it.

*Can Ulee save his business and his family at the same time?*

Peter Fonda is brilliant as the emotionally detached Ulee. He effectively portrays the struggle and turmoil his character feels over the destruction of his family. The brilliance of Fonda is seen in the way he expresses the character's emotions with his haunting eyes. You look deeply into Fonda's eyes and see the turmoil and pain his character feels. He doesn't need pages of dialogue to achieve it. Most actors would overlook a role like Ulee because it lacks that one dramatic, Oscar-friendly scene where the character makes some impassioned speech. However, Fonda is subtly amazing in every scene. His performance captivates the audience without exploding off the screen and into your face. It's a role that only a true thespian can handle.

While Fonda is the main draw, there are strong performances throughout the movie. Steven Flynn is wonderfully evil as bad guy Eddie. Instead of playing a stereotypical greedy thief, the character of Eddie is multi-dimensional. Flynn makes the character come off as an intelligent man who has taken the wrong path in life. He also shows his character to have a begrudging respect for his nemesis, Ulee.

The always solid Patricia Richardson plays the role of Ulee's neighbor and potential romantic interest, Connie Hope. While the character's name is a little too obvious, Richardson, as always, puts in a solid, not-so-obvious performance. She is a good foil for Fonda. Where his character is emotionally subdued and intensely private, Richardson makes her character more open and intrusive. She breaks through the wall of protection Ulee has built around himself.

Jessica Biel is also fantastic as teenage Casey. While the character starts as a stereotypical troubled, rebellious teen, the character evolves into a strong, maturing young lady in the face of a turbulent situation.

You kind of wonder where that talent went when you see her in run-of-the-mill comedies today.

Of course, great acting is aided by great material. Writer/director Victor Nunez creates a sensitive script that gives each character understandable motivation and an important part of the plot. Each character serves a purpose. My only quibble with the movie is questionable editing. In some scene, the cuts from one shot to another are very severe as if I looked away and missed something.

While many have probably heard of the movie, most of you never got a chance to see it. *Ulee's Gold* was not widely released and was lost in the shuffle. However, it was justifiably rewarded with many honors. Fonda was named best actor by the Golden Globes, The New York Film Critics Society and the Screen Actors Guild. The Independent Spirit Awards nominated Fonda (Best Actor), Nunez (Director and Screenplay), Richardson (Supporting Actress) and nominated the picture for best film. You probably remember that Fonda received an Oscar nomination.

# *Brassed Off*

❖

## *Starring Pete Postlethwaite, Ewan McGregor and Tara Fitzgerald*

Before he starred in the summer blockbusters like *Star Wars: The Phantom Menace, Moulin Rouge* and *Stars Wars 2: Attack of the Clones*, Ewan McGregor found himself in this heart warming tale of a small English town torn apart by impending closure of the local coal mine.

"Brassed Off" is English slang for being angry, which is the best way to describe the helplessness and disgust many of the characters feel in this movie. The men of Grimley have played in the town's brass band for over one hundred years, and worked in the coal mine for just as long. Old wounds from an earlier strike still linger and fear of financial disaster occupies the thoughts of every man, woman and child.

The workers' only escape from the drudgery of everyday life is the town's brass band. However, many members feel they must resign from the band, save money and prepare for hard times. Danny (Pete Postlethwaite) is the bandleader who refuses to let the group's tradition die, and struggles to convince other members to stay until the countrywide band competition is held. What he does not tell them is that he is ill with black lung disease and wants to win the national competition to restore pride to his beloved hometown. He also feels very strongly that the band is the heart and soul of this small mining town and, without it, there will be no sense of community.

As the band prepares for the competition, former town resident Gloria (Tara Fitzgerald) mysteriously returns to Grimley, and wishes to join the same band her grandfather played in before her. Although the band does not allow women, Gloria's superior playing ability gives them hope that they have a chance of winning the competition.

Gloria's return reignites feelings of passion in her childhood sweetheart and fellow bandmate, Andy (Ewan McGregor). However, Andy soon learns why Gloria has returned and struggles with his feelings for her and loyalty to his fellow workers.

*Will the coal mine be shut down?*

*Will the union decide to take a severance package instead of fighting to keep it open?*

*Can the band survive?*

Without a doubt, the best performance in this movie belongs to Stephen Tompkinson who plays Danny's son, Phil. Phil is a man under great pressure as he faces the loss of everything he holds dear. He is greatly in debt and running afoul of loan sharks. His wife is angry at him because he continues to play in the band, and his father pressures him into staying because he wants his son to love music as much as he does. Phil also wants to stay loyal to his fellow workers, so he speaks out against a severance package offered to the miners even though it would help his desperate financial situation. Tompkinson is captivating as we watch his steady descent into depression.

Pete Postlethwaite should also be commended for his dignified and strong performance as Danny. He wonderfully portrays his character's stoicism as his condition worsens, and brings great dignity to the character battling for his life.

Writer and director Mark Herman has put together a great movie. He brilliantly mixes scenes of the band on tour with scenes of the battles back home. The beautiful music serves as a stunning backdrop to strife, labor unrest, families arguing about their future and the union's climatic decision. He has created complex characters who face tough decisions as they try to make the best choices they can.

*Brassed Off* is a joyous, dramatic and inspirational ride. While the movie is a response to British government policies regarding the phase out of coal mining and its impact on the towns that are dependent on it, the themes and events are familiar to anyone who grew up in the Northeast and lived through the early 90's recession. I was raised in upstate New York where communities were fundamentally changed as major employers downsized or moved away altogether. An entire way of life and history disappeared as communities lost their will to survive. Lucky for us, *Brassed Off* trumpets this tight-knit community's struggle for survival.

# *Jawbreaker*

## *Starring Rose McGowan and Rebecca Gayheart*

Many modern movies tend to go for style over substance. They rely heavily on a hip attitude and a soundtrack full of smash artists to bring people into the theater, but forget that good movies have a quality screenplay and talented actors. Once in a while, you run across a movie that combines all the elements and stands out from the crowd.

*Jawbreaker* successfully combines a solid screenplay, hip and talented actors, a stylish look and a fantastic soundtrack to create an irreverent, entertaining, tongue-in-cheek dark comedy.

Courtney (Rose McGowan), Foxy (Julie Benz), Liz (Charlotte Ayanna) and Julie (Rebecca Geyhart) rule the school. These four teenage girls form the school's most envied and hated quartet. They strut down the halls, demand respect and terrorize the school's less popular students.

Courtney quietly envies Liz. She rules by fear, but Liz is loved by her fellow students for her kindness and good nature. She has earned the love and respect of some of the school's less popular students, especially, Fern Mayo (Judy Green). However, Liz still remains a part of the group because being popular is too important.

To celebrate Liz's birthday, the other three girls decide to stage a fake kidnapping of her as a joke. Unfortunately, Liz suffocates on a jawbreaker stuffed in her mouth to keep her from screaming. Since Liz's parents are on vacation for just one more day, the trio has only 24 hours to figure out how to cover it up.

## *Can the secret be kept?*

Writer/Director Darren Stein creates a wonderfully stylish movie. He dresses the characters in bright, bold, almost neon colors that jump off the screen. He uses these same colors for sets and props. Stein combines this color scheme with great use of slow motion shots and a driving soundtrack that draws on alternative rock, eighties pop and even some fifties doo-wop to form a visually and aurally stunning movie. The plot has some great twists and will leave you laughing.

Stein also delves into an interesting examination of how children change when they grow into teenagers. Many of the nerds and cool kids used to be friends in grade school, but as they grow and fall into the social structure of high school, they deny previous friendships and experiences. Some of the most interesting scenes are with Geyheart and Green sadly reminiscing over a past friendship that has fallen by the wayside. Even Green's character is representative of this behavior as she denies her entire identity once she becomes cool.

Rose McGowan is clearly the star of this film. She explodes off the screen. McGowan understands that the character is over the top and playfully relishes in her character's evilness. Her scheming and use of her own sexuality provide some of the most entertaining moments in the film. Her explanation of the cool rules will shock you with their silliness, and sadden you when you realize that many teenagers really think this way.

In February of 1999, *Jawbreaker* opened in a very limited release of just 800 theaters. In only three weeks in release, the movie grossed over $3 Million for SONY. It suffered some backlash from reviewers who compared it to a similar 80's movie, *Heathers*.

Many reviewers also put too much focus on the Marylin Manson connection. He is Rose McGowan's fiancée, and makes a brief, but anonymous unless you are looking for it, cameo appearance.

The movie is a great rental for those who are a little younger and enjoy a dark comedy. If you think your high school experience was tough, rent Jawbreaker and compare.

# *The Apostle*

## *Starring Robert Duvall and Farrah Fawcett*

Robert Duvall has been in some of the greatest movies of our time, but never seems to get the kind of recognition afforded to Jack Nicholson or Robert Redford. Duvall's resume contains some of the greatest movies in history: *To Kill a Mockingbird, M\*A\*S\*H, The Godfather* and *The Godfather II, Apocalypse Now, Network, Tender Mercies, The Natural* and *Sling Blade*. Normally, a list like that would make you a Hollywood legend, but Duvall has never been a megastar. He is a consummate professional, a workingman's actor. Instead of playing Robert Duvall in every movie, he becomes the character. He blends into the work, but would be vitally missed if he were not there.

In stunning contrast to some of his most famous roles, Duvall explodes off the screen in *The Apostle*. With great skill, Duvall serves as the writer and director as well as playing a difficult character. Duvall portrays Sonny, a flawed southern preacher. Since he was a little boy, Sonny had the gift of preaching the Lord's word. Unfortunately, he is also a deeply flawed man who has cheated on his wife and may have even stolen some money from the church collection plate.

Finally, his wife (Farrah Fawcett) tires of Sonny's problems, and takes away everything he holds dear. After being removed as pastor of his small Texas church, Sonny is lost. He turns to alcohol and begs for God to give him a sign telling him what he should do.

**Will he be able to leave his sinful past behind?**

There are some great moments in this film. Duvall's performance is legendary. His preaching ability could bring atheists to their feet. He creates a montage of fantastic scenes showing Sonny preaching to many different audiences. In one scene, Sonny and his fellow preachers engage in a preach-off, trading the microphone and compelling each other to new heights. Duvall effectively uses flashbacks to show the life Sonny has led and the events that influenced him.

*The Apostle* is a great film for actors to study Duvall. He was deservedly nominated for an Oscar and a Screen Actors Guild award. He won best actor from the Independent Spirit Awards, the LA Film Critics Association, and the National Society of Film Critics. The Independent Spirit Awards also rewarded Duvall by naming the film best film of 1997 and picked him as the best director.

# The DayTrippers

## Starring Hope Davis, Stanley Tucci, Anne Meara, Liev Shreiber and Parker Posey

*The DayTrippers* unites some of the hottest talent in independent movies for a hilarious and dramatic examination of relationships. Writer/director Greg Mottola and cast take a deep look at the relationships between parents and children, men and women, and siblings. And, when you think about it, those are the things that make us get up in the morning.

The movie opens with Eliza (Hope Davis) and Louis (Stanley Tucci) returning home from Thanksgiving with her parents and sister. This gives Louis a chance to quickly establish the overriding theme of the movie. When commenting on sister Jo's (Parker Posey) apparently loving relationship with Carl (Liev Schreiber), he states, "It's hard to tell from the outside." The rest of the movie grabs onto this idea by showing us the inside view of the various apparently happy relationships.

The next morning, after Louis departs for work and a book party, disaster strikes. Eliza finds a love note penned by Sandy, but not addressed directly to Louis. Immediately suspecting the worst, she runs to her family to seek advice about her husband's apparent infidelity with another woman. Her mother, Rita, (Ann Meara) convinces her to go into town and confront Louis. With that, the adventure begins.

Rita, Eliza's father (Pat McNamara), Carl, Jo and Eliza pile into the family station wagon bound for New York City.

### *What will they find?*

It's a simple plot, but Mottola has created one of the most enjoyable and suspenseful comedies ever. Along the way, we meet a wild cast of characters and learn more about the leading players as well. We must always be mindful that nothing is as it appears, and we are consistently surprised by the startling revelations.

The movie is a fantastic example of great screenwriting and ensemble acting. Mottola gives each character, leads as well as supporting characters, moments to shine. Each actor gets at least one scene to strut his or her stuff. These moments explain the underlying motivations of the characters as well as support the overall theme and move the plot along. Not a single minute of the 88-minute picture is wasted.

Liev Schreiber steals the show. While the other actors and actresses are fantastic, Schreiber creates the most complex character of the bunch. His character, Carl, is a pseudo-intellectual construction worker who also fancies himself to be a novelist. Carl has an oddball, stuck up opinion about everything, so we should hate him, but Schreiber and Mottola give the character a soft side that draws sympathy from the audience when his world starts to fall apart. I dare you not to laugh at the plot of his novel.

While many "discovered" Hope Davis in *Arlington Road* and *Mumford*, she has been lighting up the screen in independent films for several years. Davis is wonderful as a wife facing destruction of the marriage she holds dear. Her quiet anger and desperation contrasts beautifully with the rest of the cast, which is much more extroverted. The last scenes when she confronts Tucci are brilliant.

If you ever wondered where Ben Stiller got all that talent, look no further than his mother, Ann Meara. She is a riot as the nosey, bitchy, manipulative mother of Jo and Eliza. Her best scenes come when she takes on the role of detective to get to the bottom of the matter and the poignant closing scenes where she must confront the strained relationships she has with her husband and children. Also, Tucci, Pat McNamara, Patricia Gay Harden, Campbell Scott, Paul Herman and Marc Grapey also put in tremendous performances in limited roles. Each one is memorable for the few scenes he or she appears in.

Rent this movie immediately!

# Shall We Dance?

### Hideko Kara and Yo Tokui

Japan is better known for its production of electronics and automobiles than for films. However, one of its greatest exports is one of the sweetest films I have seen in years. Special thanks to my friend, Bob McCarson, who told me about this film a few years ago.

*Shall We Dance* stars Koji Yakusho as Mr. Sugiyama—a middle class, accountant with a wife, teenage daughter and a big mortgage. His life has become hum-drum and he has accepted his fate of working his life away to pay the bills. One day, he sees a beautiful, forlorn woman, Mai (Tamiya Kusakari) staring out the window of a dance studio. Sugiyama signs up for dance classes, so he can spend time with this beautiful instructor, but ends up dancing in a beginners' class with an older instructor, Tamako (Raiko Kusamara), and the hapless Hattori (Yo Tokui) and Tanaka (Hiromusa Taguchi).

**Will he get good enough to dance with Mai?**

**Will he start enjoying it?**

**When his wife starts thinking that he is having an affair, will she dump Sugiyama?**

At the beginning of the movie, we learn that, in Japanese culture, men and women do not engage in the public physical contact that we are used to in America due to stricter social mores. Because of this, dancing is frowned upon as embarrassing and socially inappropriate.

While I have seen several Americans who should be banned from dancing (don't wear the cut off top if you have a gut, just some advice), it is an uplifting, emotional escape.

By pursuing dance, Sugiyama, Hattori and the rest are a group of rebels defying convention to have a good time and free their souls. They live in a secret underground world. It is uplifting to watch them transform from depressed, boring sadsacks into people full of life.

The movie is full of great performances. Tokui provides welcome comic relief as the Mr. Know-It-All who tries to encourage his classmates, and Taguchi is lovable as the man who has joined the class to lose weight. However, Naoto Takenaka steals the show as Sugiyama's co-worker, Mr. Aoki—a hilariously quirky man who is lonely and insecure. I don't want to give too much away, but his sub-plot was my favorite part of the film.

You also will enjoy Yakusho's portrayal of the man who comes back to life through finding his true love—dance. He is a common man who played by the rules all of his life. However, once he has achieved the goal that society tells him he should strive for, Sugiyama is empty. It wasn't his goal. With dance, he frees himself from his worries and troubles, if only for a short time. Sugiyama has a new goal that he cares about.

*Shall We Dance* is subtitled, but don't let that scare you off. Check it out this weekend.

# *Matewan*

◆

## *Starring Chris Cooper, Kevin Tighe, and Gordon Clapp*

Every once in a while, a movie will surprise you. Maybe it was funnier than you thought or scarier. Maybe you meet a new actor that no one else knows. Or, you're just blown away by the entire package. That's what happened to me the weekend I rented *Matewan*.

Chris Cooper stars as Joe Kenehan, a union organizer for the United Mine Workers of America in the 1920's. The West Virginia coal miners are tired of the company taking advantage of them. They are forced to buy all their goods from the company store, live in company housing and work long hours in dangerous conditions for little pay. This treatment drives workers to declare a strike against the company, and Kenehan has come to recruit them into the national union.

However, things aren't that easy. The company decides to hire Italian immigrants and African Americans to replace the locals. Also, they have brought in some hired goons to change a few minds with their fists. Only their solidarity, the Mayor and the town Sheriff, Sid Hatfield (David Straitharn) can stop them.

*Will Joe be able to keep the workers together and avoid violence?*

*Will the Italians and African Americans cross the line and work as scabs?*

John Sayles did an amazing job of representing the struggles faced by the coal miners and their families in this true to history tale. In real life, Hatfield became a legendary figure in West Virginia for standing up to the Stone Mountain Coal Company and its hired goons. The event portrayed in the end of the film actually happened and started the bloodiest union battles in American history. It's a great script with many twists and turns that will keep you guessing. Sayles creates a masterpiece with just $4 Million. I don't know how he was able to recreate the West Virginia town, remote countryside and coal mines with such a low budget, but it was well worth the effort. In the end, however, the movie gets an 'A' for the cast.

Chris Cooper, best known as the evil father next door in *American Beauty*, is fantastic as the young, dedicated leader. He valiantly tries to dissuade the workers from using violence, but faces a difficult task. The frustration of being mistreated by the company and their anger at the strong arm tactics of the goons drive the group to the brink. Whether he is making a rabble rousing speech, trying to calm the miners down, or courting the widow Radner (Mary McDonnell), Cooper is able to capture the right tone and emotions for his character. He makes a controversial character very likable.

Watch for Kevin Tighe as Hickey, the lead goon. He creates a dangerously intelligent and ruthless character that serves as the perfect villain. Tighe contrasts well with Gordon Clapp's Griggs, a lackey goon who isn't very smart and falls prey to his vices. Griggs loves violence, while Hickey knows how to use it as a tool. The two are a good pair.

Three other performances also stand out. First, Nancy Mette is wonderful as Connie, the town flirt whose unrequited love for Joe is used against her later in the film. She showcases her character's naivete and desperate yearning for love and happiness in a painfully sad way that earns a big thumbs up from me. Second, David Straitharn brings quiet dignity to Sheriff Hatfield (yes, he was a part of the infamous Hatfield family that feuded with the McCoys). He doesn't give any histrionic speeches. Straitharn simply conveys his character's strength with action and a steely stare. Lastly, don't forget James Earl Jones as

Few Clothes Johnson, a leader of the African American workers who finally finds a place where he is treated like a man, instead of a slave.

Matewan is a great film and one of the forgotten masterpieces of our times.

# The Woman In Black

❖

## *Starring Adrian Rawlins and Pauline Moran*

When I mentioned that I was going to do a special section on horror movies for Halloween, Victoria Jones was insistent that I check out this selection. It was a great suggestion, and one that has caused nightmares ever since. Thanks for the good movie, but I will get revenge for the nightmares! However, if you rent the film and have nightmares, don't blame me. I warned you ahead of time.

Adrian Rawlings stars as a young lawyer in London, Arthur Kidd. He is an up-and-coming talent in his firm, but the President doesn't have much faith in him. Kidd is given a new assignment that could be a turning point in his career. He has been asked to wrap up the affairs of Mrs. Drablow, the widow of a rich client. The President usually takes care of the Drablow file, but he doesn't want to make the trip to the small seaside town. Why not?

Although the assignment will take him away from his young family for about a week, Kidd accepts and sets off to Crythin Gifford to attend the funeral, gather all relevant papers and take care of other loose ends. Along the way, everyone he encounters becomes spooked when he mentions the Drablow name. Why?

After he arrives in town, he keeps seeing a mysterious woman dressed all in black.

*What does she want?*

*Why is everyone else afraid of her?*

Everyone is afraid of her because she is freaky! In this day of high tech makeup, the woman in black frightens the strongest souls with a simple pale face and evil eyes. Pauline Moran puts in one of the greatest performances in horror movie history as she haunts Adrian Kidd everywhere he goes.

This film scares the dickens out of you because you know the action is just around the corner, just over the hill or just behind the door. I had to stop the videotape 3 times to gather myself when the action got too intense. Get ready for a wild story that continues to frighten up to the very end, and plan to take a few days to see the entire movie.

If you want a scare this weekend, check out *The Woman in Black*.

0-595-25744-5

Printed in the United States
1002500004B